Hic fuit expertus in quovis jure Robertus
L: Waldby dictus, nunc est sub marmore strictus.
Sacrae scripturae doctor fuit et geniturae;
Ingenuus medicus et plebis semper amicus.
Praesul Adurensis, post haec archas Dublinensis.

Hinc Cicestrensis, tandem primas Eborensis
Quarto kalend Junij migravit cursibus anni.
Milleni ter centum septem nonies quoque decem.
Vos precor orate quod sint sibi dona beatae
Cum sanctis vitae requiescat, et hic sine lite.

UNIVERSITY OF YORK
BORTHWICK INSTITUTE OF HISTORICAL RESEARCH

A CALENDAR
of the Register of
ROBERT WALDBY
Archbishop of York, 1397

David M. Smith

BORTHWICK TEXTS AND CALENDARS:
RECORDS OF THE NORTHERN PROVINCE 2

N.K.M.G.

in memoriam

FIRST PUBLISHED 1974

© University of York 1974

In the interests of economy this volume has been reproduced by small offset lithography. The charge made is purely to cover production costs.

CONTENTS

Frontispiece
   (memorial brass of Archbishop Waldby, Westminster
   abbey, taken from F. Drake, *Eboracum* (London, 1736),
   plate facing p.436)

Introduction   i

Abbreviations   vii

Calendar of the Register   1

General Index   51

INTRODUCTION

This volume is the first calendar to be produced in the series of Borthwick Texts and Calendars. Work is already well advanced on a calendar of the earliest surviving act book of the York High Commission Court which will appear later in the series and it is also hoped that eventually other later medieval archbishops' registers will be issued in similar form. While no calendar can ever hope to replace consultation of the original documents, at least such a publication can readily answer certain points of enquiry and can save considerable time when recourse has to be had to the original. If the present volume achieves this aim, then it has served its primary purpose.

The many admirable editions of episcopal registers published over the years by the Canterbury and York Society testify to the great wealth and variety of information contained in the registers of the late thirteenth and first half of the fourteenth centuries. Indeed, it is particularly gratifying that the first volume of an edition of the impressive York register of Archbishop William Melton (1317-1340) will appear under the Society's imprint relatively soon. Nevertheless it is equally undeniable that in general, by the end of the fourteenth century, and certainly by the fifteenth, the number of documents included in registers is considerably less and the prolixity of merely formal documents increases. In such circumstances it is arguable whether a full, critical edition is either necessary or, in these days of soaring printing costs, financially feasible. Archbishop Waldby's register which contains, if one may be permitted to borrow Professor Hamilton Thompson's comment on a similar volume, 'a halfpenny-worth of information to an intolerable deal of common form', appeared to us to be a most suitable candidate for publication in brief calendar form.

****

An Augustinian friar and a native of Yorkshire, Robert Waldby had been very closely associated with the conduct of the king's government in Aquitaine and Ireland for the greater part of his career and he had acquired the customary rewards for such faithful service to the Crown in the form of a steady progression of episcopal appointments.[1] In 1387 he received the bishopric of Aire and three years later the archbishopric of Dublin. In November 1395 he was preferred to the bishopric of Chichester but he had vacated it in less than a year. On 5 October 1396 he was translated by papal provision to the see of York vacant by the elevation of Thomas Arundel to Canterbury.[2] The temporalities of the archbishopric were assigned to him on 6 March 1396/7 [3] but he died nine months later - on 29 December 1397. [4] At the direction of King Richard II, his body was interred in Westminster abbey in the chapel of St Edmund and St Thomas the martyr.

Waldby's links with the northern province during his brief archiepiscopate could not unreasonably be described as tenuous. Apparently detained in the capital and its environs by national affairs for most of his pontificate, he deputed the day-to-day administration of his diocese to a vicar-general, master William Cawood, and to two suffragan bishops, Oswald of Whithorn and Richard of Serbia (?) (Serviensis). These archiepiscopal assistants were no strangers to the York diocese and all had seen service under Waldby's predecessors.

---

1. For the career of Robert Waldby, see A.B. Emden, A Biographical Register of the University of Oxford to A.D.1500, III, (Oxford, 1959),p.158; James Tait in the Dictionary of National Biography; J. Raine, The Historians of the Church of York and its Archbishops, II, (Rolls series, 1886), pp.427-8.

2. Calendar of Papal Letters, IV, pp.535,543.

3. Calendar of Patent Rolls 1396-1399, p.90.

4. 29 December 1397, according to his epitaph, Historians of the Church of York,II,pp.427-8; Browne Willis, Survey of Cathedrals, I, (London, 1742), p.39. Le Neve and Weever give 29 May 1397 but this is brought about by a misreading of 4th calends of January for 4th calends of June, J. Le Neve, Fasti Ecclesiae Anglicanae, (London, 1716),p.309; J.Weever, Ancient Funerall Monuments,(London, 1631), p.481, an error followed by the engraver of the print of Waldby's funeral brass (see frontispiece). T.D. Hardy's revision of Le Neve (Oxford, 1854), III,p.108; W. Stubbs, Registrum Sacrum Anglicanum, (Oxford, 1897),p.81; Emden, op.cit. and Handbook of British Chronology,(2nd ed.,1961),p.265, all record his death as occurring on 6 January 1397/8. The sede vacante register of the chapter of York commences on this day (Borthwick Institute, Reg. 5A,ff.231-231v) but it has become apparent from an examination of other vacancy registers at York that they did not necessarily begin on the day of the archbishop's demise. Since the chapter

Master William Cawood, a canon of Ripon collegiate church by 1393, had been appointed vicar-general by Archbishop Arundel in June of that year [5] and he was destined to resume these vicarial duties for a short time during the pontificate of Henry Bowet (1407-1423).[6] Richard *episcopus Serviensis* had served Archbishops Thoresby, Neville and Arundel as a suffragan [7] and his colleague, Oswald of Whithorn, appears with increasing frequency in the York registers from 1388.[8]

The register of Waldby's archiepiscopate (which is now assigned the Borthwick Institute classification reference, Reg.15) should more correctly be termed the register of his vicar-general, for the existence of another register - Archbishop Waldby's own register *extra diocesim* - is proved by the *sede vacante* records of the cathedral chapter of York. In 1397/8 a list of archiepiscopal registers handed over to the chapter by master William Cawood concludes as follows: '...Item registrum vicarii generalis reverendi in Christo patris domini Roberti Waldby nuper Eboracensis archiepiscopi, et quo ad proprium registrum dicti reverendi patris, prefatus magister Willelmus Cawod' dixit quod fuit London' in scribendo et componendo, quod quidem registrum nuncquam devenit ad manus dicti venerabilis capituli.' [9] In the vacancy after Archbishop Scrope's execution in

---

    actually issued a commission to prove Waldby's will on 6 January (ibid.,f.231v) it follows that the archbishop's death would have to have taken place some days earlier for news of it to have reached York.

5. M. Aston, *Thomas Arundel* (Oxford 1967),pp.295,310-11,395. For Cawood's life and career, see J.T. Fowler, *Memorials of the Church of SS.Peter and Wilfrid, Ripon*, II,(Surtees Society LXXVIII, 1886), pp.212-3; A. Hamilton Thompson in *Miscellanea*, II,(Surtees Society CXXVII,1927),pp.292-3; *Testamenta Eboracensia*, I,(Surtees Society IV,1836),p.395.

6. Borthwick Institute, Reg.16 (Bowet),ff.34v-35 [1415-1415/6].

7. See Borthwick Institute, Reg.11 (Thoresby), ff.379-392 *passim* [1370-1373]; Reg.12 (Neville), ff.119v-139v *passim* [1375-1383]; Reg.14 (Arundel),ff.69,71v,72 [1393/4-1396]. Bishop Richard was dead by 3 April 1398 (Reg.5A (Vacancy register), f.244v).

8. See D.E.R. Watt, *Fasti Ecclesiae Scoticanae Medii Aevi ad annum 1638*, (Scottish Record Society, new series 1, 1969),p.131; for his York activities, see Borthwick Institute, Reg.14 (Arundel), ff.10, 14v, 63-74 *passim* [1388-1396].

9. Borthwick Institute, Reg.5A (Vacancy register), f.231.

1405 there is a similar entry regarding Waldby's register <u>extra diocesim</u> [10] but after this date there is no further mention of this volume, which must now be regarded as lost.

The brief record of Waldby's pontificate still surviving at York is a slim register consisting of some eighteen parchment folios, measuring approximately $14\frac{1}{4}$" x $10\frac{1}{4}$". It comprises two gatherings: the first, of fourteen folios, contains the record of the vicar-general's diocesan administration; the second, of four folios, is devoted exclusively to the ordinations celebrated by the suffragan bishops. The register retains its original limp covers, although it has since been bound with the register of Archbishop Thomas Arundel.[11] The front cover bears the near-contemporary heading 'Registrum vicarii generalis archiepiscopi Waldeby' together with the later additions, namely 'Waldby 1396' and 'Hen.4. 8'. Inside the front cover in a seventeenth-century hand is the note 'Waldby nuper Ebor' Archiepiscopus'. One folio is left blank both at the beginning and at the end of the volume. The remaining folios have been numbered in the seventeenth century from 1 to 14 in Arabic numerals and folios 15 and 16 have modern pencil numeration. In the register there is a uniformity of handwriting and with very few exceptions marginal headings preface the registered entries. The arrangement of the subject-matter is, generally speaking, chronological and, in common with other registers of York vicars-general, no attempt is made to adhere to the divisions by jurisdiction and category which are a feature of the registers of the archbishops.[12]

---

10. Ibid.,f.259.

11. In 1930-1931, Reg.12, 13, 14, 15, 16, 17, 21 and 30 were rebound (at a total cost of £16.1s.0d.) by Ruddocks of Lincoln, at the instigation of Professor A. Hamilton Thompson and Canon C.W. Foster. On this occasion registers 14 and 15 were bound together, as were registers 17 and 21 (Borthwick Institute, DR.C&P., Diocesan Registrar's Correspondence and Letter-books 1930-1931).

12. For the York registers, see A. Hamilton Thompson, 'The Registers of the Archbishops of York' in <u>Yorkshire Archaeological Journal</u>, XXXII, (1936), pp.245-63; E.F. Jacob, <u>The Medieval Registers of Canterbury and York</u>, (St Anthony's Hall Publications 4, York, 1953). It is hoped in the not too distant future to publish <u>A Handlist of the Registers of the Archbishops of York</u> in the series of Borthwick Texts and Calendars.

This present calendar attempts to include, as far as possible, the essential information contained in each entry in the register. An exception has been made in the case of the six registered copies of wills, the contents of which have purposely not been summarised. Four have already been printed, with some abbreviation, in the Surtees Society series of <u>Testamenta Eboracensia</u>. Wills do not lend themselves easily to adequate but brief calendaring and either demand printing <u>in extenso</u> in the original form or else <u>verbatim</u> translation. It was stated earlier that the aim of this series is to make the contents of records known to interested scholars and students in a suitably concise form and to facilitate, rather than attempt to replace, consultation of the original. Obviously, if the testamentary material were to be either calendared or rendered in full, then the size of future calendars of registers would be considerably increased. The register of Waldby's successor, Richard Scrope, contains copies of twenty-four wills; that of his successor, Henry Bowet, one hundred and ten. A possible solution might be the publication of a volume of wills from the archiepiscopal registers. In such circumstances it has been decided to confine references to these wills in the calendar to the briefest details of the testator, place of residence, and date of the will.

The modern equivalent of all place names is given except in those cases where there is some doubt as to their positive identification. Personal names - even territorial surnames - have been retained in the form in which they appear in the text. Variants in the spelling of personal names have been collected together in the index and, wherever possible, modern equivalents have been given. The marginal headings of the original entries have been omitted although reference has been made to them on the few occasions when they contain additional information not in the text.

It should be remembered that all business emanates from the vicar-general of the archbishop, unless it is specifically stated otherwise.

Acknowledgements

It is a pleasant task to acknowledge my gratitude to all those who have contributed to the completion of this volume. Firstly I must thank His Grace the Archbishop of York and his Diocesan Registrar, Mr G.P. Knowles, for permission to publish Waldby's register. My deep gratitude must also be expressed to the late Mrs Norah Gurney, Professor R.M.T. Hill, Mrs D.M. Owen, Dr R.B. Dobson and Mr W.J. Sheils for reading the text and for making many valuable comments and suggestions. Their knowledge has saved me from many errors. The text was typed by Mrs M. Turner and Miss A. Cooper and I am most grateful to them for their patience in the many revisions of the typescript. Mr P. Winskill and his staff of the University Printing Unit have been, as always, most ready to help and advise at all stages in the production.

March 1974   David M. Smith

ABBREVIATIONS

Br.	Brother
l.d.	letters dimissory
O.Carm.	Carmelite
O.Carth.	Carthusian
O.Cist.	Cistercian
O.Clun.	Cluniac
O.F.M.	Franciscan
O.P.	Dominican
O.S.A.	Augustinian (Austin)
O.Semp.	Gilbertine
pa.	parish
t.	title

REGISTRUM VENERABILIS VIRI MAGISTRI WILLELMI DE CAWOD', IN LEGIBUS
LICENTIATI, REVERENDI IN CHRISTO PATRIS ET DOMINI DOMINI ROBERTI DEI
GRACIA EBORACENSIS ARCHIEPISCOPI ANGLIE PRIMATIS ET APOSTOLICE SEDIS
LEGATI, IPSO REVERENDO PATRE EXTRA SUAS CIVITATEM ET DIOCESIM IN
REMOTIS AGENTE, IN SPIRITUALIBUS VICARII GENERALIS, XXVIto DIE MENSIS
MARCII ANNO DOMINI MILLESIMO CCCmo NONAGESIMO VIImo ET TRANSLACIONIS
DICTI REVERENDI PATRIS ANNO PRIMO INCEPTUM

folio

1 9 March 1396/7 London

  Commission from Archbishop Waldby to master William Cawode,
  licentiate in both laws, authorising him to exercise the
  office of vicar-general in spirituals in the city and diocese
  of York during the archbishop's absence, with the power of
  canonical coercion. Collations of benefices in the
  archbishop's patronage, the issue of letters dimissory on the
  production of titles of dignities, benefices and other offices
  within the archiepiscopal jurisdiction, the granting of
  dispensations in accordance with the constitution <u>Cum ex eo</u>
  and for the celebration of divine service in private oratories
  and other such matters affecting the archbishop's prerogative
  were all specifically reserved to Waldby.*

1 31 March 1397 Ripon

  Commission to master Thomas Laundelles appointing him Official
  of the archbishop's spiritual jurisdiction of Hexham during
  pleasure, with powers of enquiry and correction in respect of
  offences committed by the archbishop's subjects within the
  jurisdiction and of cognizance of all spiritual cases requiring
  judicial investigation, with the power of canonical coercion.

1 1 April 1397 Ripon

  Mandate to the official of the archdeacon of York ordering him
  to induct Adam de Popilton, formerly rector of Hackford in
  the diocese of Norwich, or his proctor, into corporal
  possession of the rectory of Thornton in Craven, to which he
  had been presented by Beatrice, lady de Roos, by reason of an
  exchange of benefices with Rowland Quik.

---

* In the corroboration clause of this commission, it is stated that
  since Waldby did not yet possess a York seal, he was using for the
  present his seal as archbishop of Dublin.

<u>folio</u>

1-1v   19 March 1396/7   South Elmham

Certification by William Carleton, doctor of both laws, vicar-general of Henry [Despenser], bishop of Norwich, of his execution of the commission of the chapter of York <u>sede vacante</u> (given in full and dated at York, 22 February 1396/7) for the exchange of benefices between Adam de Popilton, rector of Hackford, and Rowland Qwhyk, rector of Thornton in Craven. He had instituted Adam to Thornton in Craven in the person of his proctor, John Hayhard, and on the presentation of Beatrice, lady de Roos [Rosse], having first received the resignation of Rowland Qwhyk [Quik].

1v   1 April 1397   Ripon

Letter to the clergy of the peculiar jurisdiction of Hexham and Hexhamshire ordering them to warn publicly those persons withholding charters, rolls, evidences, indentures, rents, books and any other moveable goods belonging to the archbishop, to restore them to the steward or the bailiff of the archbishop, upon pain of greater excommunication.

1v   4 April 1397   [no place given]

Memorandum of the appointment of Thomas Barneby, vicar of the prebend of Saltmarsh in the collegiate church of Howden, to perform the office of penitentiary in Howdenshire for one year.

1v   4 April 1397   [no place given]

A similar commission of one year's duration granted to Roger Stevynson, parochial chaplain of Hemingbrough, to hear the confessions of his parishioners.

1v   6 April 1397   [no place given]

A similar commission granted to Robert Sparowe, parson ('persona') in the cathedral church of York, to perform the office of penitentiary in the archdeaconry of York for one year.

folio		
1v	6 April 1397	[no place given]

A similar commission of one year's duration granted to John Darnyngton, parson ('persona') in the cathedral church of York, to hear the confessions of parishioners in the archdeaconry of Richmond.

1v-2	6 April 1397	Ripon

Commission to Br. Oswald, bishop of Whithorn, to act as a suffragan in the city of York and the archdeaconries of York, Richmond and Nottingham during pleasure. His episcopal duties were specified as the dedication, consecration and reconciliation of churches, chapels and churchyards, the suspension of high altars if unconsecrated and the dedication, consecration and reconciliation of these and fixed and portable altars, the collection of procurations (with power to employ ecclesiastical censure against those failing to pay), the confirmation of children and adults, the consecration of chalices and patens, the blessing of ecclesiastical vestments and ornaments, and the conferment of all minor orders on suitable candidates after due examination.

2	7 April 1397	Ripon

Letter of institution of William Farman, chaplain, to the provostship of Kirkby Overblow, vacant by the resignation of John Whitewell.
Patron: Henry de Percy, earl of Northumberland.

Memorandum that a mandate for induction was directed to the official of the archdeacon of York on the same day.

2	6 April 1397	Ripon

Memorandum that letters dimissory were granted to John Ingylby, acolyte, to receive further orders from any Catholic bishop.

2	7 April 1397	[no place given]

Memorandum of the appointment of Robert Louthorp, vicar in the collegiate church of Beverley, to perform the office of penitentiary for one year.

folio

2   9 April 1397   Ripon

Memorandum that letters dimissory were granted to John at Well, acolyte, to receive further orders from any Catholic bishop.

2   9 April 1397   Ripon

Absolution <u>ad cautelam</u> of William Fedyrstonhalgarth and Adam Clerk from sentences of excommunication incurred by the killing of William Stubbys, a tenant of the liberty of Hexham. They swore that they would go to the Papal Curia in person to obtain absolution within a year, or else would obtain, by papal authority, the benefit of absolution in form of law.

2   9 April 1397   Ripon

Memorandum of a commission to the rector of Stanhope, in the diocese of Durham, or his parochial chaplain to absolve <u>ad cautelam</u> John Rowsyde, Robert Wellesede, William Merley, John Taylour, Adam Wylson, John de Rokhop, William Blakburn, Robert Hedryngton, John Trotter, Robert de Halle and Robert Fedyrstonhalgh from sentences of excommunication for murder* on the same condition as above.

2   11 April 1397   Ripon

Mandate to Alexander, prior of Hexham, authorising him to enjoin salutary penance for Br. William de Bolton, a rebellious canon of his house (printed in full in <u>The Priory of Hexham, its chroniclers, endowments and annals</u>, ed. J.Raine, I (Surtees Society, XLIV, 1864), no.lxix, p.xc).

---

* This additional information is obtained from the marginal heading to the entry.

folio

2-2v   11 April 1397   Ripon

Letter to Sir John Claveryng, knight, bailiff of the liberty of Hexham. When instructions were given to the clergy of the peculiar jurisdiction to warn those persons withholding charters rolls, evidences and other muniments belonging to the archbishop to restore them, upon pain of greater excommunication, to the bailiff or the archbishop's steward, it was never the vicar-general's intention that the bailiff should proceed against Alexander, prior of Hexham and the archbishop's chancellor in the liberty. The muniments in the prior's custody had been committed to him by Archbishop Arundel and were to remain with him until the arrival of the archbishop's steward.

2v   12 April 1397   Ripon

Letter of institution of Richard Wetewang, chaplain, to the rectory of Dunnington, vacant by the resignation of William Farman.
Patron: Henry de Percy, earl of Northumberland.

Memorandum that a mandate for induction was directed to the official of the archdeacon of Cleveland on the same day.

2v   15 April 1397   Ripon

Memorandum that letters dimissory were granted to William Doun, acolyte, to receive further orders from any Catholic bishop in England.

2v   18 April 1397   Ripon

Execution of a commission from Francis [Carboni], cardinal priest of St Susanna and papal penitentiary (given in full and dated at St Peter's, Rome, 10 December 8 Boniface IX [1396]). William Goteson, layman, and Matilda Lange, his wife, had formerly obtained a dispensation on apostolic authority, having contracted matrimony notwithstanding that they were related within the fourth degree of affinity. However they had since petitioned the penitentiary about the validity of this dispensation, William having earlier had carnal knowledge of a woman related to his wife Matilda in the third and fourth degrees of consanguinity. In accordance with a declaration made by Pope Clement VI in similar instances, the penitentiary commissioned the vicar-general to declare the previous dispensation valid, just as if mention of the third degree had been made in it.

5

folio

2v-3   24 April 1397   Ripon

Commission to master Ralph Oudeby, bachelor of laws, to investigate and report upon the state of the priory of Hexham and its members and to enquire about the observance by the prior of visitation injunctions issued in the time of Archbishop Arundel by master John de Suthwell (printed in full in The Priory of Hexham, I, no.lxx, pp.xci-xcii).

3   22 April 1397   Ripon

Letter of institution of John Masun [Mason] of Poppleton, clerk, to the rectory of Moor Monkton, vacant by the resignation of Peter de Alberwyk.
[no patron given]

Memorandum that a mandate for induction was directed to the official of the archdeacon of York on the same day.

3   23 April 1397   Ripon

Memorandum of a commission to the abbot of Whalley, authorising him to receive the vow of chastity of Emmota, widow of Sir Ralph de Ipr[e], knight, and to bestow the veil and mantle upon her.

3   17 April 1397   Eltham

Commission from Archbishop Waldby to master William Cawode, licentiate in both laws, canon of Ripon and Official [sic] of York, authorising him to proceed in the matter of an exchange between John Middelton, prebendary of Stanwick in the collegiate church of Ripon, and John Den [Deen], rector of Brandsby.*

3   21 April 1397   Ripon

Letter of collation of the prebend of Stanwick in the collegiate church of Ripon to John Deen, priest, on the resignation of John Middelton, by reason of an exchange of benefices.

---

* The Dublin seal was still being used by the archbishop.

folio

3   21 April 1397   Ripon

           Mandate to the chapter of Ripon ordering them to induct and
           install John Deen, or his proctor, as prebendary of Stanwick.

3v   21 April 1397   Ripon

           Letter of institution of John Middelton, priest, to the
           rectory of Brandsby, on the resignation of John Deen, by
           reason of an exchange of benefices.
           Patron: Marmaduke de la Ryvere, esquire.

           Memorandum that a mandate for induction was directed to the
           official of the archdeacon of Cleveland on the same day.

3v   29 April 1397   Ripon

           Memorandum that a licence was granted to John de Richemund of
           Ripon to have divine service celebrated in an oratory in his
           house for one year.

3v   4 May 1397   York

           A similar licence granted to Elizabeth Brygham and her son
           John for two years.

3v   4 May 1397   York

           A similar licence granted to Emmota Swynflet of the parish of
           Drax for two years.

3v   4 May 1397   York

           A similar licence granted to John Wenslay, citizen of York,
           for one year.

3v   4 May 1397   York

           A similar licence granted to John Thornholm, esquire, for two
           years.

7

<u>folio</u>

3v   4 May 1397   York

A similar licence granted to William Wannesford for three years.

3v   Friday before the feast of the Annunciation [23 March] 1396/7

Will of Robert Cooke of Hexham (printed in part in <u>Testamenta Eboracensia</u>, I (Surtees Society, IV, 1836), p.214).

3v   5 May 1397   York

Memorandum of the probate of the will of the abovenamed. Administration of his goods was granted to the executors named in the will.

3v-4   17 April 1397   Eltham

Commission from Archbishop Waldby to master William de Cawod, licentiate in laws, canon of Ripon, authorising him to exercise the office of vicar-general in spirituals in the city and diocese of York during the archbishop's absence, with the power of canonical coercion. On this occasion his vicarial powers included the issue of licences for the celebration of divine service in private oratories and the appointment of penitentiaries. Collations of benefices in the primate's patronage, the issue of letters dimissory on the production of titles of dignities, benefices and other offices within the archiepiscopal jurisdiction, the granting of dispensations in accordance with the constitution <u>Cum ex eo</u>, and matters affecting the seducers of nuns and those breaking into the archbishop's parks together with such other business concerning the archbishop's prerogative were all specifically reserved to Waldby.*

4   5 May 1397   York

Memorandum that a licence was granted to Hugh Seton to have divine service celebrated in his manor-house at Turnham Hall [pa. Hemingbrough] for one year.

---

*   The Dublin seal was still being used by the archbishop.

folio

4   5 May 1397   York

A similar licence granted to Richard Aglum of Beverley for one year.

4   7 May 1397   York

Memorandum of a dispensation for bastardy granted on papal authority to John Hoton, clerk, of the York diocese.

4   5 May 1397   York

Letters testimonial, issued after an inspection of Archbishop Arundel's register, certifying that Robert Craven, acolyte, had been ordained subdeacon by Br. Richard, _episcopus Serviensis_ and suffragan of Archbishop Arundel, in the conventual church of St Leonard's hospital, York, on 5 June 1395*, and deacon by the same bishop in York Minster on 18 December 1395** to the title of the cathedral church of York.

4   9 May 1397   York

Memorandum that a licence was granted to John Heton of Steeton to have divine service celebrated in an oratory in his house.

4   10 May 1397   York

Memorandum that letters dimissory were granted to Richard Flynt, of the York diocese, scholar, enabling him to be ordained by any Catholic bishop in England to any minor or holy orders, which he had not yet received.

4   10 May 1397   York

Memorandum that a licence was granted to Sir Robert Hilton, knight, to have divine service celebrated in his manor-houses within the diocese of York for one year.

---

* Borthwick Institute, Reg.14 (Arundel), f.71v.

** No record of this ordination survives in Archbishop Arundel's register.

folio

4   10 May 1397   York

A similar licence granted to Henry Naylston, priest, to have divine service celebrated in his house at Clifton for one year.

4   10 May 1397   York

A similar licence granted to William Risum to have divine service celebrated in his house at Rysome [pa. Holmpton] for one year.

4   10 May 1397   York

A similar licence granted to master Anthony of St Quintin, to have divine service celebrated in his rectory at Hornsea and his manor-house at Haisthorpe [pa. Burton Agnes] for **one** year.

4   10 May 1397   York

Letters testimonial, issued after an inspection of Archbishop Arundel's register, certifying that master John de Siggeston, deacon, was ordained priest by Br. Oswald, bishop of Whithorn and suffragan of Archbishop Arundel, in the church of St Michael-le-Belfrey, York, on 9 March 1391/2* to the title of his church of Brantingham.

4   10 May 1397   York

Memorandum that a licence was granted to the prioress and nuns of Wallingwells to choose Br. Richard de Warkesop, subprior of Worksop, as their confessor for two years.

4   10 May 1397   York

Memorandum that a licence was granted to Richard Malton, rector of Thornton Dale, to farm his church for two years to Walter de Wandesford and John Pokethorp, chaplains, and Thomas Wandesford, layman.

---

* Borthwick Institute, Reg.14 (Arundel), f.64v.

folio

4   15 May 1397   York

Memorandum that a licence was granted to Nicholas Sheffelde, esquire, to have divine service celebrated in his manor-house at Landmoth [pa. Leake] for two years.

4v   10 May 1397   [no place given]

Memorandum that a licence was granted to Robert Curtays, chaplain of the chantry of St German in the parish church of Aldbrough, to celebrate private masses for the living and the dead for one year.

4v   10 May 1397   [no place given]

A similar licence granted to John Cawthorn, rector of a mediety of High Hoyland, for one year.

4v   10 May 1397   York

Memorandum that a licence was granted to Godfrey, perpetual vicar of Gisburn in Craven, to be absent from his living for one year for fear of death.

4v   10 May 1397   [no place given]

Memorandum of a commission to Roger Gudhall, rector of Bainton, to receive the purgation of Idonea, the widow of William Pynder of Bainton, of a charge of complicity in the death of her husband, who was mortally wounded by an unknown assailant. She was said to have consented to his death and to have planned it by placing a long tent* into William's head as far as the brain and by removing four bones from his head.

---

*   '... ponendo unum longum tentum in capud ipsius Willelmi usque ad cerebrum...' 'Tentum' has been rendered as 'stake' (Yorkshire Archaeological Journal, XXV, (1920), p.119) but I am inclined to translate it as 'tent' - OED. 'A roll or pledget, usually of soft absorbent material, often medicated, or sometimes of a medicinal substance, formerly much used to search and cleanse a wound or to keep open or distend a wound, sore or natural orifice.' Presumably Idonea had attempted, without success, some rudimentary first-aid.

folio

4v　　　10 May 1397　　[York]

　　　Memorandum that a letter was sent to the aforementioned rector of Bainton ordering him to excommunicate those persons defaming Idonea in respect of her husband's death.

4v　　　10 May 1397　　York

　　　Memorandum that a licence was granted to Nicholas Grene, perpetual vicar of Rothwell, to farm his church for three years to John Harwode, chaplain, and Thomas Manchestr[e], layman and citizen of York.

4v　　　10 May 1397　　York

　　　Memorandum that a licence was granted to Thomas Sheffelde, esquire, to have divine service celebrated in his house at Braithwell for one year.

4v　　　10 May 1397　　York

　　　Letters testimonial, issued after an inspection of Archbishop Arundel's register, certifying that Peter Axiholme, acolyte, was ordained subdeacon by Br. Oswald, bishop of Whithorn and suffragan of Archbishop Arundel, in the chapel of St Mary and the Holy Angels, York, on 17 December 1390 to the title of his vicarage in Wells [cathedral]*.

4v　　　11 May 1397　　The Archbishop's Palace, York

　　　Memorandum to the effect that, in the presence of the vicar-general, John de Lyndale, Thomas Gunnays and Andrew Blendale, the executors of the will of Thomas de Etton, late rector of Huggate, paid five and a half marks to John Appilton, rector of Gilling in Rydale, and John Garton, the proctors of master Robert de Appilton, rector of Huggate, in full payment for the repair of the rectory buildings and received an acquittance. Witnesses: John Rednes, chaplain, and John Cawode.

---

* 'ad titulum vicarie sue in Well''- unfortunately it is impossible to confirm definitely that this is Wells cathedral, since the ordination lists for 1390 are now missing.

<u>folio</u>

4v   12 May 1397   York

Notification to the rural dean of Bulmer relaxing the sequestration of the goods of William Farman, the former rector of Dunnington, since he had given sufficient security for the payment of ten marks to Richard de Wetewang, the present rector, for the repair of certain defects in the rectory from the time of his incumbency.

4v   17 May 1397   [no place given]

Memorandum that a licence was granted to John Segefeld, rector of Stokesley, to be absent from his living for one year and to farm his benefice.

4v-5   12 May 1397   York

Certification by the chapter of York (the dean being in distant parts) of the execution of the vicar-general's commission (given in full and dated at York, 11 May 1397) for the exchange of benefices between William Maundeville, rector of Leathley, and John de Campsale, vicar of Wadworth. The chapter had instituted John de Campsale to the rectory of Leathley, on the resignation of William Maundevile, and on the presentation of the prior and convent of Healaugh Park.

5   12 May 1397   York

Mandate to the rural dean of Otley ordering him to induct John de Campsale, formerly vicar of Wadworth, or his proctor, into corporal possession of the rectory of Leathley, to which he had been instituted on the resignation of William Maundevyle, by reason of an exchange of benefices.
Patrons: the prior and convent of Healaugh Park.

5   23 May 1397   York

Memorandum of a dispensation, granted at the instance of the papal penitentiary, to William Rycale of East Cottingwith and Juliana Tombarne permitting them to contract matrimony, notwithstanding that they were related within the fourth degree of consanguinity.

folio

5   17 June 1397   York

Memorandum that a licence was granted to master Richard de Killum, skilled in law, rector of a mediety of Gedling, to be absent from his living for one year and to farm his benefice. He was dispensed from attendance at synods.

5   23 May 1397   York

Letter of institution of John Whatton, chaplain, to the rectory of Goxhill, vacant by the resignation of Robert Selby, by reason of an exchange of benefices.
Patron: Ralph Leley.

Memorandum that a mandate for induction was directed to the official of the archdeacon of the East Riding on the same day.

5   23 May 1397   York

Letter of institution of Robert Selby, chaplain, to the perpetual chantry of St Mary, Sibthorpe, vacant by the resignation of John Whatton, the last warden of the chantry, by reason of an exchange of benefices.
Patrons: Gilbert Notbroun, Henry Pepircorn, Richard Padlay and John Howby, chaplains of the chantry of St Mary, Sibthorpe.

Memorandum that a mandate for induction was directed to the official of the archdeacon of Nottingham on the same day.

5   23 May 1397   York

Memorandum that a licence was granted to the hospital of St Thomas the Martyr outside Micklegate Bar, York, to have divine service celebrated in the hospital for three years.

5   23 May 1397   York

A similar licence granted to Marmaduke Darell of Sessay for one year.

folio

5   25 May 1397   Ripon

Memorandum of the correction of Br. Richard Hemeswell and Br. William Wodhorn, canons of the priory of Hexham, both having confessed to the crime of fornication. The salutary penance enjoined by the vicar-general was suspended for unspecified causes ('certis de causis ipsum moventibus') (printed in The Priory of Hexham, I, no.lxxi, p.xciii).

5   25 May 1397   Ripon

Memorandum that a licence was granted to Emmota, widow of Ralph de Ipre, to have divine service celebrated at suitable places within the diocese of York for one year.

5v   25 May 1397   Wellhaugh

Certification by Walter [Skirlaw], bishop of Durham, of his execution of the commission of Archbishop Waldby (given in full and dated at London, 27 April 1397*) for the exchange of prebends between master John Danby, prebendary of Crophill and Oxton (alias Oxton Prima Pars) in the collegiate church of Southwell, and master Thomas de Weston, prebendary of Twiford in St Paul's cathedral, London, and prebendary of Darlington church. On the archbishop's authority and on that of Robert [Braybrooke], bishop of London, Walter had collated the prebend of Crophill and Oxton to master Thomas de Weston.

5v   29 May 1397   Ripon

Mandate to the chapter of Southwell ordering them to admit and install master Thomas de Weston as prebendary of Crophill and Oxton.

5v   31 May 1397   Ripon

Memorandum that a licence was granted to John Markham, king's justice, to have divine service celebrated in his manor-house for one year.

---

* From the tenor of the corroboration clause, it would appear that Archbishop Waldby possessed a York seal by this date. A photograph of Waldby's York seal is to be found in G. Benson, Later Medieval York, (York, 1919),p.60.

15

folio

6 31 May 1397   Ripon

A similar licence granted to John Fletwode to have divine service celebrated in his house at Fieldplumpton [pa. Kirkham] for one year.

6 12 May 1397   York

Mandate to the rural dean of Bulmer to make enquiries about non-resident rectors of livings within his deanery. They were to be warned to return to their benefices within a time to be specified by the rural dean and proceedings were to be taken against those who did not comply. A list of names of these non-resident rectors was to be furnished to the vicar-general before next Trinity [17 June 1397]. Enquiries were to be made in respect of those monastic clergy with cure of souls and others who sold their tithes to laymen and of those who farmed them before they had been separated from the nine parts. The vicar-general was also to be informed of their names.

6 6 June 1397   Ripon

Memorandum of the probate of the will of William son of Roger de Thorp of Burnsall. Administration of his goods was granted to the executors named in the will.

6 7 June 1397   Ripon

Memorandum that a licence was granted to master Peter de Bolton, rector of Scrayingham, to be absent from his living for one year and to farm his benefice.

6 12 June 1397   Ripon

Commission, with power of canonical coercion, to master Geoffrey de Pikeryng, professor of Holy Writ, abbot of Byland, and John de Deen, canon of Ripon, to carry out a visitation of Arden priory, to correct any excesses and defects which were discovered, and to remove the prioress if it appeared that her faults required it, appointing a new prioress in her place.

folio		
6	16 June 1397	York

Memorandum that a licence was granted to Sir William Ergum, knight, to have divine service celebrated in his hospice at Beverley for one year.

| 6 | 16 June 1397 | York |

A similar licence granted to John Dysny, esquire, to have divine service celebrated in his house at Fosham [pa. Aldbrough] for one year.

| 6 | 17 June 1397 | York |

A similar licence granted to Miles de Stapilton to have divine service celebrated in his manor-house at Carlton [by Snaith] for one year.

| 6 | 17 June 1397 | York |

A similar licence granted to the inhabitants of Asselby [pa. Howden] to have divine service celebrated in the chapel of Asselby for one year.

| 6 | 18 June 1397 | York |

Memorandum of the probate of the nuncupative will of Thomas Bakster of Rotherham. Administration of his goods was granted to his executors, Robert de Hyll and John de Retteford, chaplains.

| 6-6v | 18 June 1397 | York |

Memorandum of the acquittance of the abovenamed executors of the will of Thomas Bakster.

17

folio

6v   18 June 1397   York

Memorandum that letters dimissory were granted to John de Whynfell, acolyte, to receive all further orders from any Catholic bishop.

6v   19 June 1397   York

Memorandum that a licence was granted to the prior and convent of North Ferriby to have divine service celebrated for one year in a suitable oratory within Cotys in Waldyng [? Coates and Walden, pa. Barnoldswick].

6v   19 June 1397   York

A similar licence to Richard Clyff, donzel, to have divine service celebrated in his manor-house at Cliffe [Clyff] for one year.

6v   19 June 1397   York

A similar licence granted to Thomas Ravynthorp for an oratory in his house at Ravensthorpe [pa. Felixkirk] for one year.

6v   19 June 1397   York

A similar licence granted to Margaret, widow of Sir Richard de Roclyff, knight, to have divine service celebrated in her manor-house for one year.

6v   21 June 1397   York

A similar licence granted to Sir Thomas Roth, knight, to have divine service celebrated in his manor-house at Thorpe by Bedale [? Thorpe Perrow] for one year.

folio		
6v	26 June 1397	Ripon

Memorandum that a licence was granted to John Appilton, rector of Gilling in Rydale, to be absent from his living for two years and to farm his benefice.

| 6v | 3 June 1397 | |

Will of Alice Mustardmaker of Ripon (printed in part in Testamenta Eboracensia, I, p.221).

| 6v | 27 June 1397 | Ripon |

Memorandum of the probate of the will of the abovenamed. Administration of her goods was granted to the executor named in the will.

| 6v | 27 June 1397 | Ripon |

Memorandum of the probate of the will of Alice, wife of Robert Skynner of Ripon. Administration of her goods was granted to her husband.

| 6v | 28 June 1397 | Ripon |

Memorandum of the acquittance of the executor of Alice Mustardmaker of Ripon.

| 6v-7 | 30 May 1397 | York |

Inspeximus by Archbishop Waldby of a charter of the bailiffs and commonalty of Scarborough (given in full and dated on the feast of St Dunstan 20 Richard II [19 May 1397] in the common hall at Scarborough and witnessed by Peter de Castro Novo, monk of the Cistercian order and warden of the church of Scarborough, Theobald his fellow-monk, John de Gowsell, perpetual vicar of Scarborough, Robert de Bucton, chaplain of the chantry of St James, Robert de Newby, John de Rithir) founding, with the consent of King Richard II and the archbishop, a perpetual chantry at the altar of the Blessed Virgin Mary in the parish church of St Mary, Scarborough in honour of Jesus Christ and the Blessed Virgin Mary and all saints and for the souls of Emery Edwyn and Reginald Milner and for the souls of ancestors and benefactors and of all the faithful departed and for the commonalty of Scarborough, both living and dead. The chantry was endowed with certain lands,

19

folio

6v-7 possessions and rents in the town of Scarborough, granted in separate charters. The right of presentation to the chantry was vested in the commonalty of Scarborough in perpetuity. They were to present a suitable chaplain to the archbishop <u>sede plena</u> or the dean and chapter of York <u>sede vacante</u> (or the chapter of York in the dean's absence) for admission to the chantry within a fortnight after the vacation of the benefice. If they neglected to use their right of patronage within the appointed time, the presentation devolved upon the archbishop <u>sede plena</u> and the dean and chapter of York <u>sede vacante</u>. The perpetual vicar of Scarborough was to induct the chaplain into corporal possession of his chantry. It was laid down that the chantry chaplain was to celebrate or cause to be celebrated by another, the mass of Our Lady at the altar of the Blessed Virgin Mary every day, except on the principal feast-days, and also on ordinary days he was to say the office for the dead and the commendation for the souls of those previously named in the foundation charter. He was personally responsible for the condition of the books, chalice, vestments and ornaments of the chantry and also for the repair and maintenance of the houses and buildings belonging to the chantry and he was required to rebuild them at his own expense, if it ever proved necessary. The chaplain was charged with the performance of a solemn obit each year, to be celebrated within the octaves of St Agnes the martyr, for the souls of Henry de Roston [Ruston], senior, and his wife Margery. The chaplain was also to celebrate two anniversaries, one for the souls of Henry de Ruston, senior, and Margery his wife within the octaves of St Agnes, the other for William Masun and Richard de Askam, chaplains, within the octaves of St Laurence the martyr. At every feast of nine lessons, except for reasonable cause, he was to be in choir, at matins, masses, vespers and processions, wearing a surplice. He was also obliged to repair the second house on the west by the churchyard of the charnel as often as was necessary. The house was always to be occupied by two, three or four poor persons and the chaplain was to give them six shillings and eightpence each year, either in fuel or in clothing or in the repair of the property, this sum being expended out of the rent of the house, once in the possession of John Wadmain, which Adam Clerk granted to the chantry. Provision was made for the removal of the chaplain if ever he was convicted of offences in respect of his responsibilities in these matters or for any outrageous crime. The chaplain was to possess all the lands, rents and tenements belonging to the chantry on the conditions specified in the burgesses' charter. The archbishop gave his approval to the foundation of the chantry.*

---

* For a brief notice of this document, see N.A.H. Lawrence, <u>Fasti Parochiales</u>, III (Yorks. Arch. Soc. Record Series, CXXIX, 1967), p.112. Whether the chantry was founded for Emery Edwyn and Reginald Milner, or for Emery, Edwin and Reginald Milner is not absolutely clear, although the former is supported by the Chantry Survey of Edward VI.

folio

7   23 June 1397   York

Letter of institution of Richard Askam, chaplain, to the
perpetual chantry at the altar of the Blessed Virgin Mary in
the parish of Scarborough.
Patrons: the bailiffs and commonalty of Scarborough.

Memorandum that a mandate for induction was directed to the
perpetual vicar of Scarborough on the same day.

7v   10 May 1397   London

Commission from Archbishop Waldby to master William de Cawode,
licentiate in laws, canon of Ripon and vicar-general, reciting
a writ of King Richard II (given in full and dated at Eltham
12 April 1397)*, commanding the archbishop to summon
Convocation of the northern province to be held in York Minster
on the Friday after the feast of St John ante portam latinam
[11 May]. Since the time allowed in the royal writ for the
summoning of Convocation was very short, the archbishop
postponed the date of the meeting until 19 June. The vicar-
general was to convoke a meeting of Convocation to be held
in York Minster before the archbishop's commissaries on that
day, the bishops of the province to be represented by proctors,
the deans, abbots, priors, archdeacons and provosts to appear
in person, the chapters to be represented by one proctor, the
clergy of each archdeaconry and peculiar jurisdiction by two
proctors.

7v   31 May 1397   London

Commission from Archbishop Waldby to master William de Cawode,
canon of Ripon and vicar-general, the abbot of St Mary's, York,
master John de Newton treasurer of York, master Thomas de Dalby
archdeacon of Richmond, master William de Feryby archdeacon of
the East Riding, master Nicholas de Feryby canon of York,
master Thomas Walworth canon of York and master Alan Newark,
bachelor of laws, with the power of canonical coercion. Since
Waldby was unable to attend the Convocation of the province to
be held in York Minster on 19 June, he authorised the
recipients of his commission to be present at the session in
his name and to demand a tenth of temporalities and
spiritualities for the king's use in the defence of his realm,
and also to exact a grant of a halfpenny in the pound on every
benefice for the expenses of the abbot of Nonantola, the
ambassador of Pope Boniface IX. They were to come to an
agreement with the prelates and clergy then present over the
terms of payment of these two subsidies.

---

* Calendar of Close Rolls 1396-1399, p.118

folio

7v   9 July 1397   Southwell

Letter of institution of William Chaster, chaplain, to the perpetual chantry of the Fraternity of the Blessed Virgin Mary in the parish church of St Mary Magdalen, Newark, vacant by the resignation of John Halton, by reason of an exchange of benefices.
Patron: Richard Seynell, warden of the Fraternity of the Blessed Virgin Mary at the altar of All Saints in the parish church of Newark.

Memorandum that a mandate for induction was directed to the official of the archdeacon of Nottingham on the same day.

7v-8   9 July 1397   Southwell

Letter of institution of John Halton, chaplain, to the perpetual chantry in the chapel of Melton [pa. Welton], vacant by the resignation of William Chaster, by reason of an exchange of benefices.
Patron: William de Feryby, donzel.

Memorandum that a mandate for induction was directed to the custodian of the spirituality of Howden and Howdenshire on the same day.

8   18 June 1397   York

Dispensation on account of canonical irregularity granted on papal authority* to Thomas Karlow, a professed monk of the Cluniac priory of Pontefract.**

8   16 July 1397   Southwell

Memorandum of the probate of the will of Helen, wife of John Horncastell of Farnsfield. Administration of her goods was granted to her husband.

---

*   This information is obtained from the marginal heading to the entry.
**   The nature of the irregularity is not specified. Br. Thomas Carlow[e], monk of Pontefract, was ordained subdeacon on 5 June 1397 (Borthwick Institute, Reg.14 (Arundel), f.71v) and deacon on 16 June 1397 (see p.41). It is just possible that this dispensation was in some way connected with his ordination. He was ordained priest on 13 March 1399/1400 (Borthwick Institute, Reg.16 (Scrope), f.155v).

folio

8   23 July 1397   Southwell

Letter of institution of Robert Hemyngburgh, chaplain, to the vacant perpetual vicarage of Skipwith, with the burden of residing in person and ministering continuously in accordance with the legatine constitution.
Patrons: the prior and convent of Durham.

Memorandum that a mandate for induction was directed to the custodian of the spirituality of Howdenshire on the same day.

8   24 July 1397   Southwell

Letter of institution of John son of Henry Glover, chaplain, to the perpetual vicarage of Kirkby in Cleveland, vacant by the death of William de Aton, with the burden of residing in person and ministering continuously in accordance with the legatine constitution.
Patrons: the abbot and convent of Whitby.

Memorandum that a mandate for induction was directed to the official of the archdeacon of Cleveland on the same day.

8   26 July 1397   Southwell

Memorandum of the probate of the will of the wife of Robert Squier of Nottingham. Administration of her goods was granted to the executor named in the will.

8   2 August 1397   Southwell

Memorandum of the probate of the will of Henry de Stabyll of Farnsfield. Administration of his goods was granted to his wife, the executrix named in the will.

8-8v   14 July 1397   London

Commission from Archbishop Waldby to master William de Cawode, his vicar-general, authorising him to proceed in the matter of an exchange of prebends between master Thomas la Warr[e], prebendary of Grindal in the cathedral church of York, and master Thomas de Weston, prebendary of Crophill and Oxton (alias Oxton Prima Pars) in the collegiate church of Southwell.

23

<u>folio</u>

8v   6 August 1397   Southwell

Letter of collation of the prebend of Grindal in the cathedral church of York to master Thomas de Weston, licentiate in laws, archdeacon of Durham, on the resignation of master Thomas la Warre (in the person of Thomas Barneby, his proctor), by reason of an exchange of prebends. This letter was drawn up as a public instrument and subscribed by master Robert Blundell, notary public.
Witnesses: master Robert de Broughton, rector of Colkirk in the diocese of Norwich, John Rednes, priest, of the York diocese, William Auncel, donzel, of the Lincoln diocese, and John Strech, donzel, of the Worcester diocese.

8v   6 August 1397   Southwell

Mandate to the cathedral chapter of York ordering them to install master Thomas de Weston, or his proctor, as prebendary of Grindal.

8v   6 August 1397   Southwell

Letter of collation of the prebend of Crophill and Oxton in the collegiate church of Southwell to master Thomas la Warr[e] (in the person of Thomas Barneby his proctor) on the resignation of master Thomas de Weston, by reason of an exchange of prebends.

Memorandum that a mandate for installation was directed to the chapter of Southwell on the same day.

8v   6 August 1397   Southwell

Memorandum of the protestation (recited in full) made before the vicar-general in the hall of his house at Southwell by Thomas Barnby, proctor of master Thomas la Warr[e]* in respect of the above exchange, reserving his right to resume the prebend of Grindal, in the event of his being dispossessed of the Southwell prebend as a result of any defect in the legal position of his predecessors as holders of that prebend.

---

* In this entry master Thomas la Warre is additionally described as a canon of Lincoln and prebendary of Lafford [Sleforde], in the same way as master Thomas de Weston is styled archdeacon of Durham in the entry at the top of this page. This is the source of the error in <u>Le Neve: Fasti Ecclesiae Anglicanae 1300-1541 : Lincoln Diocese</u>, (London, 1962),p.72, when Weston is listed as prebendary of Lafford by reason of an exchange with Warre. His name should be deleted from the list of prebendaries.

folio		
9	Monday before the feast of St James [23 July] 1397	

Will of Elias de Sutton, rector of Harthill.

9	8 October 1397	[no place given]

Memorandum of the acquittance of his executors.

9	10 August 1397	Southwell

Memorandum of the probate of the will of the abovenamed. Master Richard Rasyn, bachelor of laws, was empowered to commit the administration of his goods to the executors named in the will.

9-9v	16 June 1397	Westminster

Commission from Archbishop Waldby to master William de Cawode, his vicar-general, authorising him to receive from Richard Derby, who was worn out and broken with old age and sickness, the resignation (simple or by reason of exchange), cession, or voidance by any other means of the archdeaconry of Nottingham. He was to confer the vacant archdeaconry upon John de Notyngham, rector of Cottingham. Provision was to be made for the retiring archdeacon for the rest of his life out of the revenues of the archdeaconry.

9v	10 August 1397	Southwell

Letter of collation of the archdeaconry of Nottingham in the cathedral church of York to John de Notyngham, on the resignation of Richard Derby.

9v	10 August 1397	Southwell

Mandate to the cathedral chapter of York ordering them to install John de Notyngham, or his proctor, into corporal possession of the archdeaconry.

<u>folio</u>			

9v   11 August 1397   Southwell

Mandate to the abbots, priors, clergy and people of the archdeaconry of Nottingham to obey John de Notyngham, the new archdeacon.

9v   13 August 1397   Southwell

Memorandum of the dispensation for bastardy granted to William de Oxton, of York diocese, scholar, on the authority of Francis [Carboni], cardinal priest of St Susanna and papal penitentiary, enabling him to be promoted to all orders and to hold a benefice, even with cure of souls.

9v   13 August 1397   [no place given]

Memorandum that letters dimissory were granted to the aforesaid William de Oxton, clerk, to receive all minor and holy orders from any Catholic bishop in England.

9v   Saturday after the feast of Holy Trinity [23 June] 1397

Will of Sir Richard Byron, knight (printed in part in <u>Testamenta Eboracensia</u>, I, p.222).

9v   15 August 1397   Southwell

Memorandum of the probate of the will of the above-named. Administration of his goods was granted to the executors named in the will.

10   14 August 1397   Nettleham

Certification by John [Buckingham], bishop of Lincoln, of his execution of the vicar-general's commission (given in full and dated at Southwell, 12 August 1397) for the exchange of benefices between Thomas Wilforde [Wylford], rector of Walesby, and John Wayte, rector of Hickling. He had instituted Thomas Wilforde to Hickling, on the presentation of John Grey, lord of Sandiacre, having first received the resignation of John Wayte.

folio

10   15 August 1397   [no place given]

Memorandum that a mandate for the induction of Thomas Wilford into corporal possession of the rectory of Hickling was directed to the official of the archdeacon of Nottingham.

10   13 August 1397   Southwell

Assignment to Richard de Westderby, on his resignation of the archdeaconry of Nottingham in the person of his proctor Thomas del Acres, chaplain, of a pension from the revenues of that archdeaconry. Since the annual income of the archdeaconry did not exceed one hundred pounds, the pension was fixed at eighty silver marks to be paid each year out of the revenues of the archdeaconry, by John de Notyngham, the present archdeacon, in two equal instalments, to wit at Martinmas and Whitsun, for the rest of Richard's life. In the event of default of payment, provision was made for John's subsequent excommunication and the imposition of a fine of ten pounds to be given to Richard de Westderby.

10   20 August 1397   Southwell

Commission to John Wryght of Nottingham to administer the goods of Robert son of William Danyell of Nottingham, deceased.

10   20 August 1397   Southwell

Memorandum of the dispensation for bastardy granted to Thomas Wolton, clerk, of York diocese, on the authority of Francis [Carboni], cardinal priest of St Susanna and papal penitentiary, enabling him to be promoted to all holy orders and to hold a benefice.

10v   20 August 1397   Southwell

Letter of institution of William Spycer, chaplain, to one of the seven perpetual chantries in Holy Trinity college, Pontefract.
Patron: Sir Robert Knolles, knight, founder of the college.

folio

10v   20 August 1397   Southwell

Letter of institution of John Parlyngton, chaplain, to one of the seven perpetual chantries in Holy Trinity college, Pontefract.
Patron: Sir Robert Knolles, knight, founder of the college.

10v   20 August 1397   Southwell

Letter of institution of John Stretton, chaplain, to one of the seven perpetual chantries in Holy Trinity college, Pontefract.
Patron: Sir Robert Knolles, knight, founder of the college.

10v   Memorandum that a mandate was directed to the official of the archdeacon of York on the same day ordering him to induct the three chaplains into corporal possession of their respective chantries.

10v   23 August 1397   Southwell

Letter of collation of the archdeaconry of Nottingham in the cathedral church of York to John de Notingham, chaplain, on the resignation of Richard de Westderby.

Memorandum that a mandate for installation was directed to the cathedral chapter of York on the same day.

10v   [undated]

Protestation made before the vicar-general and other witnesses, by John de Notingham, rector of Cottingham, in respect of the collation of the archdeaconry of Nottingham. He intended to retain his rectory of Cottingham with the archdeaconry by virtue of a dispensation for plurality from Pope Boniface IX.

10v-11   30 August 1397   Southwell

Memorandum of a dispensation granted on papal authority to Thomas Stapilton, layman, and Joan Umfray, permitting them to contract matrimony, notwithstanding that they were related within the third and fourth degrees of consanguinity.

folio

11   1 September 1397   Southwell

Memorandum of the probate of the will of Lucy, wife of Richard Broculstow of Edingley. Administration of her goods was granted to her husband.

11   1 September 1397   Southwell

Letter of institution of William de Strykland, chaplain, in the person of Thomas de Scawceby, clerk, his proctor, to the prebend of Howden in the collegiate church of Howden, vacant by the death of master Michael Sergeaux.
Patrons: the prior and convent of Durham.

Memorandum that a mandate for induction was directed to the custodian of the spirituality of Howden and Howdenshire on the same day.

11   2 September 1397   Southwell

Letter of institution of master Richard Kendale, chaplain, to the perpetual vicarage of Greasley, vacant by the death of Robert [de Tymersholt], with the burden of residing in person and ministering continuously in accordance with the legatine constitution.
Patrons: the prior and convent of Beauvale.

Memorandum that a mandate for induction was directed to the official of the archdeacon of Nottingham on the same day.

11   2 September 1397   [no place given]

Memorandum of the probate of the will of Robert de Tymersholt, vicar of Greasley. Administration of his goods was granted to the executors named in the will.

11   12 September 1397   Southwell

Letter of institution of William Keworth, chaplain, to a perpetual chantry in the chapel of St James, Melton [pa. Welton], vacant by the resignation of John de Haloughton.
Patron: William de Feriby, donzel.

Memorandum that a mandate for induction was directed to the custodian of the spirituality of Howdenshire on the same day.

29

folio

11   17 September 1397   Southwell

Memorandum of the probate of the will of Robert Martill of Chilwell [pa. Attenborough]. Administration of his goods was granted to Agnes his widow and William Chillwell, chaplain, the executors named in the will.

11   18 September 1397   Southwell

Memorandum of the probate of the will of John del Stabyll of Farnsfield. Administration of his goods was granted to Joan his widow, the executrix named in the will.

11   20 September 1397   Southwell

Memorandum that a licence was granted to master Thomas Revell, rector of Hockerton, to be absent from his living for one year and to farm his benefice.

11   25 September 1397   Ripon

Letter of institution of Peter Sherman, chaplain, to the perpetual vicarage of Fishlake, vacant by the resignation of Robert Gaynesburgh, by reason of an exchange of benefices, and with the burden of residing in person and ministering continuously in accordance with the legatine constitution. Patrons: the prior and convent of Durham.

Memorandum that a mandate for induction was directed to the official of the archdeacon of York on the same day.

11v   25 September 1397   Ripon

Letter of institution of Robert de Gaynesburgh to the perpetual vicarage of Maltby, vacant by the resignation of Peter Sherman, by reason of an exchange of benefices, and with the burden of residing in person and ministering continuously in accordance with the legatine constitution.* Patron: the prioress of Arthington.

Memorandum that a mandate for induction was directed to the official of the archdeacon of York on the same day.

---

* At one point in this letter of institution the scribe has confused the benefices being exchanged and Fishlake is written in error for Maltby.

folio

11v   30 September 1397   Ripon

Licence to the abbot of Rufford to farm, for two years, the revenues of the parish church of Rotherham and, for four years, the tithes of Masbrough [pa. Rotherham], both of which were appropriated to his monastery.

11v   4 October 1397   York

A similar licence granted to the prior of the cathedral church of Durham permitting him to farm, for one year, the revenues of the churches of Fishlake, Ruddington and Bossall, appropriated to his house. He was also dispensed with personal attendance at the archbishop's synod for these churches during this period.

11v   4 October 1397   York

Memorandum of a licence granted to Thomas Kellow, rector of Lythe, to be absent from his living for two years and to farm his benefice.

11v   5 October 1397   York

Letter of institution of Henry Holmeton, chaplain, to the perpetual chantry of St Mary in the church of Goxhill, vacant by the resignation of Robert de Thirnom.
Patron: John de Goushill, vicar of Scarborough.

Memorandum that a mandate for induction was directed to the official of the archdeacon of the East Riding on the same day.

11v   22 September 1397   London

Memorandum of the dispensation, granted in accordance with the constitution Cum ex eo, to master William Norton, rector of Tanfield, to study in England for three years and to farm his benefice for that period.*

---

* This dispensation was presumably granted by Archbishop Waldby, cf. p.8 [vicar-general's commission].

31

<u>folio</u>

11v   9 October 1397   York

    Memorandum of the dispensation for bastardy granted on papal
    authority to William de Cave, clerk, of York diocese, enabling
    him to be promoted to all holy orders and to hold an
    ecclesiastical benefice, even with cure of souls.

11v   5 October 1397   York

    Memorandum of the dispensation for bastardy granted on papal
    authority to John [son of] Ralph Coterell, clerk, of York
    diocese, enabling him to be promoted to all orders and to hold
    an ecclesiastical benefice.

11v   5 October 1397   York

    Memorandum of the dispensation for bastardy granted on papal
    authority to John Croke, clerk, of York diocese, enabling him
    to be promoted to all orders and to hold an ecclesiastical
    benefice.

11v   10 October 1397   York

    Memorandum that letters dimissory were granted to Adam de
    Grene, clerk, of York diocese, to receive all minor and holy
    orders, which he had not yet taken, from any Catholic bishop
    in England.

11v   10 October 1397   York

    Memorandum that letters dimissory were granted to Richard
    Esyngton, clerk, of York diocese, to receive all minor and
    holy orders, which he had not yet taken, from any Catholic
    bishop in England.

11v   [undated]

    Note that the vicar-general adjourned Convocation of the
    province of York, fixed by Archbishop Waldby for 10 October
    1397, because it was not established what had been done or
    granted in Convocation of Canterbury. It was to meet on 13
    February 1397/8, unless it became clear before that date what
    had been granted in the southern province.

folio

12   10 October 1397   York

Admission of Br. Thomas de Hoveden, a canon of the Gilbertine priory of St Mary, Ellerton [on Spalding Moor], to the custody of the parish church of Aughton, in accordance with papal indults granted to the order, and on the presentation of the prior and convent of Ellerton, to whom the benefice was appropriated.

12   12 October 1397   York

Memorandum of the dispensation for bastardy granted on papal authority to Br. John Stafford, priest, a professed canon of the Augustinian priory of Guisborough, enabling him to minister as a priest and to be appointed to all offices and administrations of his order short of the dignity of abbot.

12   19 September 1397

Will of Emmota Raby of Cawood.

12   11 October 1397   York

Memorandum of the probate of the will of the abovenamed. Administration of her goods was granted to the executors named in the will.

12   13 October 1397   London

Memorandum of the dispensation, granted by Archbishop Waldby in accordance with the constitution <u>Cum ex eo</u>, to Adam Wygan, subdeacon, rector of the parish church of St Saviour, York, enabling him to study in England for one year, without being obliged to proceed to further orders.

12   18 October 1397   York

Memorandum that letters dimissory were granted to Richard Thesedale, acolyte, of York diocese, to receive all holy orders, which he had not yet taken, from any bishop in England.

<u>folio</u>

12   18 October 1397   York

Memorandum that letters dimissory were granted to William Layburn, acolyte, of York diocese, to receive all holy orders, which he had not yet taken, from any bishop in England.

12   26 October 1397   York

Letter of institution of William de Askby, chaplain, to a mediety of the rectory of Eakring.
Patron: William de Roos, lord of Hamlake [i.e. Helmsley].

Memorandum that a mandate for induction was directed to the official of the archdeacon of Nottingham on the same day.

12-12v   21 September 1397

Will of Sir Ralph de Hastinges, knight (printed in part in <u>Testamenta Eboracensia</u>, I, pp.216-219).

12v   8 November 1397   York

Memorandum that a licence was granted to Thomas Kyrketon, rector of Terrington, to be absent from his living for three years and to farm his benefice. He was dispensed with personal attendance at York synods but was obliged to send a proctor.

12v   9 November 1397   York

Memorandum that letters dimissory were granted to Thomas Esyngwald, of York diocese, scholar, to receive all minor and holy orders, which he had not yet taken, from any Catholic bishop in England, on production of a sufficient title.

12v-13   9 November 1397   York

Letter of institution of John Goxhill, chaplain, to the perpetual chantry of the Blessed Virgin Mary in the parish church of Scarborough, vacant by the resignation of Richard Askam, by reason of an exchange of benefices.
Patrons: the bailiffs and commonalty of Scarborough.

Memorandum that a mandate for induction was directed to the official of the archdeacon of the East Riding on the same day.

folio		

13   9 November 1397   York

    Letter of institution of Richard de Askeham, chaplain, to the perpetual vicarage of Scarborough, vacant by the resignation of John de Gouxhill by reason of an exchange of benefices.
    Patron: King Richard II, the temporalities of the alien priory of the church of St Mary, Scarborough being in his hands, by reason of the French war.

    Memorandum that a mandate for induction was directed to the official of the archdeacon of the East Riding on the same day.

13   13 November 1397   York

    Letter of institution of John Spryngot, chaplain, to the rectory of Harthill, vacant by the death of Elias Sutton.
    Patrons: the prior and convent of St Pancras, Lewes.

    Memorandum that a mandate for induction was directed to the official of the archdeacon of York on the same day.

13   14 November 1397   York

    Memorandum of the dispensation, granted at the instance of Francis [Carboni], cardinal priest of St Susanna and papal penitentiary, to John Waleys, layman, and Christine Kilner, permitting them to contract matrimony, notwithstanding that they were related on both sides within the fourth degree of consanguinity, and declaring their future issue legitimate.

13   17 November 1397   York

    Letter of institution of John Kyndenesse, priest, of York diocese, to the vacant rectory of Warmsworth.
    Patron: Gocelin Daynale.

    Memorandum that a mandate for induction was directed to the official of the archdeacon of York on the same day.

folio

13   26 November 1397   York

Letter of institution of Henry Wresyll, chaplain, to the
perpetual chantry at the altar of St John the Baptist in
the church of St Peter the Little, York, vacant by the death
of John de Pykton.
Patrons: Robert Assburn, rector of the parish church of St
          Peter the Little, York, John de Beverlay, Alan de
          Hamerton, John de Danby and William de Dowdale,
          parishioners of the aforesaid church.

Memorandum that a mandate for induction was directed to the
official of the archdeacon of York on the same day.

13   31 December 1397*   York

Memorandum that letters dimissory were granted to John
Fysshelak, scholar, of York diocese, to receive all orders
from any Catholic bishop in England.

13   5 December 1397   York

Memorandum that a licence was granted to Robert Duffeld,
rector of Keighley, to be absent from his living for a year
and to farm his benefice. He was dispensed with personal
attendance at York synods but was obliged to send a proctor.

13-13v   13 December 1397   Ripon

Commission to John de Popilton, vicar choral of the cathedral
church of York, to induct Thomas Popilton, priest, or his
proctor, into corporal possession of the prebend in the chapel
of St Mary and the Holy Angels, York, vacant by the
resignation of William de Neuton. The archbishop's letter of
collation (given in full) is dated at Westminster on
28 November 1397.

---

* From its position in the register, the date of this entry is
  possibly a scribal error.

folio

13v   18 December 1397   Ripon

Letter of institution of Br. Henry de Brammelay, canon of Worksop priory, in the person of master Robert Laghton his proctor, to the perpetual vicarage of Sheffield, vacant by the elevation of Br. Roger de Upton as prior of Worksop, and with the burden of residing in person and ministering continuously in accordance with the legatine constitution.
Patrons: the prior and convent of Worksop.

Memorandum that a mandate for induction was directed to the official of the archdeacon of York on the same day.

13v   On 14 January 1397/8, in the chapter-house of York Minster, master William de Cawod, the vicar-general, relinquished his office and delivered the archbishops' registers, which he had in his custody, and his seal of office into the hands of the chapter, on the death of Robert Waldby, archbishop of York.

Et sic finit Registrum

14   ORDINATIONS CELEBRATED BY BR. OSWALD, BISHOP OF WHITHORN AND SUFFRAGAN OF ARCHBISHOP WALDBY, IN THE CONVENTUAL CHURCH OF HOLY TRINITY, MICKLEGATE, YORK, ON 7 APRIL 1397.

Subdeacons

Alan de Hilton to t. of St Mary's hospital, Bootham, York, by l.d.
John Addisun to t. of the collegiate church of Ripon.
John Ingilby to t. of a mediety of the church of Eckington.
Br. Alan Wartr[e], O. Carm.
Br. William de Skelton.
Br. Adam Swyneshede.

Deacons

William Spencer to t. of Clementhorpe priory, by l.d.
Richard Brott to t. of the collegiate church of Ripon.
John Quynton to t. of the collegiate church of Ripon.
Robert Kembe to t. of Gokewell priory.
John Masun to t. of St Mary's hospital, Bootham, York.

folio

14   Deacons   cont.

Henry Polles to t. of the collegiate church of Ripon.
William Frysnay to t. of Swine priory.
Thomas Brown to t. of patrimony.
John Marchall to t. of St Oswald's priory, Nostell.
Br. Nicholas de Midilton, O. Carm.
Br. John Spowndon, O. Carm.

Priests

William Flecher to t. of Hampole priory.
Robert Barker to t. of Ellerton priory.
Thomas Gaythill of Kirk Hammerton to t. of Nun Monkton
    priory for all orders.
William Meldy to t. of Swine priory.
John Lunde to t. of Clementhorpe priory.
Henry Twynan, of Carlisle diocese, by l.d., to t. of
    Sherburn hospital.
Thomas Robynson, of Durham diocese, by l.d., to t. of
    St Mary's hospital, Bootham, York.

ORDINATIONS CELEBRATED BY BR. OSWALD, BISHOP OF WHITHORN
AND SUFFRAGAN OF ARCHBISHOP WALDBY, IN THE CONVENTUAL CHURCH
OF HOLY TRINITY, MICKLEGATE, YORK, ON 21 APRIL 1397.

14   Subdeacons

Thomas Sutton to t. of St Mary's hospital, Bootham, York,
    for all orders.
Peter Ormesby, of Lincoln diocese, to t. of the collegiate
    church of Beverley, by l.d.
John Barker to t. of Sinningthwaite priory.
William Cawode to t. of St Leonard's hospital, York, for
    all orders.

Deacons

Thomas Wyndell of Poppleton to t. of Clementhorpe priory.
Thomas Manneby to t. of Sherburn hospital.
Thomas Killom to t. of his vicarage in the cathedral church
    of York.
John Ingilby to t. of a mediety of the church of Eckington.

folio

14   Priests

John Kyrkandris, of Carlisle diocese, to t. of Holmcultram
    abbey, by l.d.
John Porter, of Durham diocese, to t. of Kepier hospital, by
    l.d.
William Routh to t. of the collegiate church of Beverley.
William Lunde to t. of the collegiate church of Beverley.
Richard Beswyk to t. of the collegiate church of Beverley.
Henry Polles to t. of the collegiate church of Ripon.
John Quynton to t. of the collegiate church of Ripon.
Robert Feriby to t. of his vicarage in the cathedral church
    of York.
Thomas Brown to t. of patrimony.

ORDINATIONS CELEBRATED BY BR. OSWALD, BISHOP OF WHITHORN AND
SUFFRAGAN OF ARCHBISHOP WALDBY, IN THE CHURCH OF ST LEONARD'S
HOSPITAL, YORK, ON 16 JUNE 1397.

Acolytes

John de Mydelton.   Thomas Martynson.
John de Hoton.   Edmund Cunstabyll.
John Smyth of Catwick.   John Lasyng.
John Coterell.   Thomas Gamyll.
John Sowleby.   John de Bampton.
Roger Selow.   William Halsted.
Thomas Brygman.   Thomas Parmeter.
Robert Cateryk.   John de Allerton.
Robert Calthorn.   John de Ormesby.
William Salflet.   Richard Gardner.
John Wodhaw.   John Holme de Dent.
John Huson.   Thomas de Allerton.
William Marshall of Tadcaster.   Thomas Rembon.
John Man de Heton.   Br. William de Harum.
John Bewyk.   Br. John Otteley, O. Carm.
Robert Tadcastr[e].   Br. John Worcestr[e], O.Carm.

Subdeacons

Thomas Frawnkelayn to t. of Shelford priory for all orders.

14v   John son of John de Elmesale of Swinefleet to t. of Selby
    abbey for all orders.
William Smyth of Hook to t. of Selby abbey.
Robert Chawmbyrlayn of Seamer to t. of Shelford priory.
Henry Illyngworth to t. of Sawley abbey.
John de Midelton to t. of the collegiate church of Ripon.
Robert Hall of Kneeton to t. of Newbo abbey.

39

folio

14v		Subdeacons	cont.

    Robert Bothumsell to t. of Welbeck abbey for all orders.
    John Crayk to t. of Selby abbey for all orders.
    William Walker to t. of Kirkstall abbey.
    John Gaynesburgh, of Lincoln diocese, by l.d., to t. of the
        collegiate church of Beverley.
    Robert Estryngton to t. of Selby abbey for all orders.
    John Martill of Walton to t. of Sinningthwaite priory.
    John Spicer to t. of St Oswald's priory, Nostell.
    John Elmesall to t. of Cartmel priory for all orders.
    master Robert Camerton to t. of patrimony.
    John Rowclyff to t. of St Andrew's priory, York.
    William son of Peter de Brakken to t. of Watton priory.
    Robert Laverok to t. of Clementhorpe priory.
    John Sproxton to t. of Moxby priory.
    John Taliour of Weighton to t. of Selby abbey.
    Richard de Harwode to t. of St Leonard's hospital, York.
    Robert Eglysclyff, of Durham diocese, to t. of Neasham
        priory, by l.d.
    Thomas Gemme of Haddlesey to t. of Selby abbey.
    John de Dalton to t. of St Oswald's priory, Nostell.
    William Mayre to t. of Swine priory.
    John Suthiby of Burton to t. of Warter priory.
    Robert Mounte to t. of Furness abbey.
    Thomas Barton to t. of Neasham priory.
    Richard Bennok to t. of Easby abbey.
    Richard Gardiner, of Durham diocese, to t. of Egglestone
        abbey, by l.d.
    Thomas Belbyrby to t. of Coverham abbey.
    Robert de Halton to t. of Cartmel priory.
    John Warton to t. of Cockersand abbey.
    Br. Simon Billysthorp, canon of Welbeck.
    Br. John Sleford, monk of Byland.
    Br. John Kylburn, monk of Byland.
    Br. John Pykeryng, monk of Byland.
    Br. John Synington, monk of Byland.
    Br. Peter de Kendale, canon of Coverham.
    Br. William de Kexby, O.P.
    Br. William de Kyrkeby, O.Carth. of Hull.
    Br. Thomas Waplyngton, O.Carth. of Hull.
    Br. Thomas Wyghall, O.Carm.
    Br. William Harum, O.P.
    Br. John Keleby, monk of Whalley, O.Cist.
    Br. Robert Otryngton, monk of Whalley, O.Cist.
    Br. John Wetherby, monk of Whalley, O.Cist.
    Br. Robert Farmlaw, monk of Whalley, O.Cist.
    Br. Thomas Rysselay, monk of Whalley, O.Cist.
    Br. Gerard Skelton, monk of Whalley, O.Cist.
    Br. William Whallaye, monk of Whalley, O.Cist.
    Br. John Blakburn, monk of Whalley, O.Cist.

folio

14v   **Deacons**

Thomas Sutton to t. of St Mary's hospital, Bootham, York, for all orders.
William Fox to t. of Hampole priory for all orders.
John Whytby to t. of Wilberfoss priory.
John Austyn, of Carlisle diocese, to t. of William de Dacr[e], lord of Gilsland, for all orders, by l.d.
John Bakster to t. of St Mary's hospital, Bootham, York.
Robert Wryght of Fenton to t. of St Andrew's priory, York, for all orders.
John Altoftes to t. of St Oswald's priory, Nostell.
John Brown to t. of Wilberfoss priory for all orders.
Thomas Holm to t. of Clementhorpe priory for all orders.
Thomas Maulay to t. of Watton priory for all orders.
Thomas Rose de Bernston to t. of Wilberfoss priory for all orders.
Richard Cotes to t. of Roche abbey for all orders.
John Estwete to t. of Felley priory for all orders.
John Fillyngham to t. of Shelford priory for all orders.
John Wryde to t. of Warter priory for all orders.
William Cawode to t. of St Leonard's hospital, York.
John Layburn to t. of Clementhorpe priory.
John Dagett to t. of Malton priory for all orders.
John Smyth of Normanton to t. of Shelford priory.
Alan de Hilton, of Glasgow diocese, to t. of St Mary's hospital, Bootham, York, by l.d.
Richard Pyrle to t. of Gokewell priory for all orders.
Thomas Cotys, of Durham diocese, to t. of Swine priory, by l.d., for all orders.
John Roklay to t. of St Andrew's priory, York, for all orders.
Simon Marflete to t. of the collegiate church of Beverley for all orders.
Robert Coteler to t. of the collegiate church of Southwell.
John Skelton to t. of St Leonard's hospital, York.
John Mopp to t. of St Leonard's hospital, York.
Thomas Norham, of Durham diocese, to t. of Alnwick abbey, by l.d.
John Addeson to t. of the collegiate church of Ripon.
Henry Jervous to t. of the cathedral church of York.
Br. Thomas Carlow, monk of Pontefract, O.Clun.
Br. Richard Devyas, monk of Pontefract, O.Clun.
Br. Robert Gargrave, monk of Sawley, O.Cist.
Br. Nicholas Clowe, monk of Sawley, O.Cist.
Br. Benedict de Clyfton, canon of Welbeck.
Br. John de Wortelay, canon of Welbeck.
Br. Robert Hesilden, O.F.M. of Richmond.

15   Br. William Haliden, O.F.M. of Richmond.
Br. William Skelton, O.Carm.
Br. Adam Swynshevide, O.Carm.

folio

15   Priests

John Clowcroft, of Durham diocese, to t. of Sherburn
    hospital for all orders, by l.d.
John Grysmer, of Carlisle diocese, to t. of William Bland,
    esquire, by l.d., for all orders.
Richard Tolston to t. of Healaugh Park priory for all orders.
Robert Grome to t. of Watton priory for all orders.
Robert Benet to t. of Mattersey priory for all orders.
Henry Colman to t. of Meaux abbey for all orders.
John Cowldon to t. of the collegiate church of Beverley.
Robert Brown to t. of Upholland priory.
John Clerk de Wymton to t. of Broadholme priory for all orders.
Stephen Maukyn to t. of Meaux abbey for all orders.
Thomas Wode to t. of the prior and convent of Durham for
    all orders.
John Hasard to t. of Mattersey priory for all orders.
John Masun of Poppleton to t. of his church of Moor Monkton,
    York diocese.
Thomas Wyndell to t. of Clementhorpe priory for all orders.
William Buk to t. of Watton priory for all orders.
John Hedon to t. of Mattersey priory for all orders.
Richard Brott to t. of the collegiate church of Ripon.
John Hardegyll, of Durham diocese, to t. of William de
    Billyngham, donzel, by l.d.
Robert Keme to t. of Gokewell priory for all orders.
Robert Marshall to t. of St Oswald's priory, Nostell.
Robert Raper to t. of Watton priory.
William Almanbury to t. of Delapré abbey, Leicester.
Robert Jors to t. of Torksey priory.
Thomas Kyllum to t. of the cathedral church of York.
Simon Ledys to t. of the cathedral church of York.
Br. William de Northwell, canon of Shelford.
Br. William de Watton, canon of Watton, O. Semp.
Br. John de Shalford, canon of Watton.
Br. John Pleselay, canon of Bolton.
Br. John Gosner, canon of St Oswald, Nostell.
Br. William de Orberye, canon of St Oswald, Nostell.
Br. Robert Wellys, O.F.M. of Newcastle.
Br. John Chadburn, O.P. of York.
Br. John Rayly, O.P. of York.
Br. John Byrden, O. Carm. of York.
Br. Robert Duffelde, O.S.A. of York.
Br. Richard Ebyrston, monk of Kirkstall.
Thomas Mannely to t. of Sherburn hospital.
William del Stabyll to t. of Coverham abbey.
John Wencelawe to t. of Easby abbey.   Rich[mond] in margin.
John Gryssyngham to t. of Cartmel priory.
Br. John Synnyngton, canon of Easby.
Br. Thomas Baglay, canon of Easby.

42

folio

15   ORDINATIONS CELEBRATED BY BR. OSWALD, BISHOP OF WHITHORN AND SUFFRAGAN OF ARCHBISHOP WALDBY, IN THE CONVENTUAL CHURCH OF HOLY TRINITY, MICKLEGATE, YORK, ON 22 SEPTEMBER 1397.

Acolytes

Thomas de Bolton of Pontefract.
Richard Tesedale.
John Freston of Holderness.
Adam Patson of Weighton.
John Marshall.
John Esyngwolde.
Robert Knayton.
John Hoton of Bedale.
John Midelham of York.
John Harpeham of Barrowby.
William Gentylman of
    Eaglescliffe.
Robert de Alta Ripa
William Carter of Tawton.
Laurence Gargrave.
Br. William Hovyngham of
    Calder, O. Cist.
Br. Richard Thwaythes of
    Furness, O. Cist.
Br. Robert Oliver, O.P.
    of York.
Br. Philip de Botylstane.
Br. William de Esyngwalde.
Br. Thomas de Sutton.
Br. William Thryntoft.
Br. Thomas Barry.

Subdeacons

Robert Banaster to t. of Kirklees priory.
Robert son of William Frer[e] to t. of Killingwoldgraves
    hospital.
Thomas Swanland to t. of the cathedral church of York.
Robert Snoll to t. of Watton priory.
Thomas Eglysclyff, of Durham diocese, to t. of Neasham
    priory, by l.d.
William Lekynfeld to t. of Swine priory.
Henry de Feriby to t. of the collegiate church of Beverley.
John Taylour of Tickhill to t. of Roche abbey.
Richard Brygg to t. of Newstead in Sherwood priory.
William de Halstede, of Coventry and Lichfield diocese, to
    t. of Sawley abbey, by l.d.
Thomas Hall of Melton to t. of Clementhorpe priory.
Henry Graysothen to t. of Louth Park abbey.
William de Pathorn to t. of Warter priory.
Robert Catryk to t. of Keldholme priory.
Thomas Parmeter of Barnbrough to t. of Hampole priory.
Robert son of Richard Smyth of Besthorpe to t. of Rufford abbey.
William de Westyrdall to t. of Clementhorpe priory.
Richard de Campsall to t. of Ulverscroft [Ulcroft] priory.
John Hughson of Helmsley to t. of Keldholme priory.
John Palmer to t. of Rosedale priory.
Thomas Baylers to t. of his church of Hawton, York diocese.
William Wellys to t. of Wilberfoss priory.
William de Gressyngham to t. of Sawley abbey.

folio

15v   Subdeacons   cont.

Thomas Preston, of Durham diocese, to t. of Moxby priory, by l.d.
John de Aghen, to t. of St Leonard's hospital, York.
Br. Thomas Sellestorn, O. Cist.
Br. William de Wartr[e], canon of Warter.
Br. Robert Blake, O.S.A. of York.
Br. Thomas Yrchestr[e], O.S.A.
Br. Thomas de Carleton, canon of Newstead in Sherwood.
Br. William Boston, O.Carm. of Doncaster.
Br. John Otlay, O. Carm. of Doncaster.
Br. William Thirletoft, O. Carm. of Doncaster.
Br. Thomas Barry, O. Carm. of Doncaster.
Br. Alan de Hert, O.P. of York.
Br. Thomas de Segesfeld, O.P. of York.
Br. Thomas de Myrtford, O.P. of York.
Br. Henry Godeworth, O.P. of York.
Br. Robert Rudstan, canon [sic] of Calder.
Br. Thomas de Skelton, canon [sic] of Calder.
Br. William Hovyngham, canon [sic] of Calder.
Br. Richard Thwates, monk of Furness.
Br. Robert Oliver, O.P.

Deacons

John Ivun to t. of the collegiate church of Southwell for all orders.
John Wakefeld, to t. of the cathedral church of York.
John Crayk to t. of Selby abbey.
William Walker to t. of Kirkstall abbey for all orders.
Richard Gardiner, of Durham diocese, to t. of Egglestone abbey, by l.d.
Thomas Newham to t. of his church of Long Newton, Durham diocese.
Adam Fynmer to t. of Warter priory for all orders.
Robert Bothumsell to t. of Welbeck abbey for all orders.
Henry Yllyngworth to t. of Sawley abbey.
John de Midelton to t. of the collegiate church of Ripon, for all orders.
William son of Peter Brakken to t. of Watton priory for all orders.
master Robert Camerton, of Carlisle diocese, to t. of patrimony, by l.d.
John Elmesale to t. of Cartmel priory for all orders.
John Sproxton to t. of Moxby priory for all orders.
John Spycer to t. of St Oswald's priory, Nostell, for all orders.
Robert Estryngton to t. of Selby abbey for all orders.

folio

15v   Deacons   cont.

Robert Eglysclyff, of Durham diocese, to t. of Neasham priory, by l.d., for all orders.
Thomas Frawnkelan to t. of Shelford priory for all orders.
Robert Chammbyrlan to t. of Shelford priory for all orders.
Richard Harwode, of Coventry and Lichfield diocese, to t. of St Leonard's hospital, York, by l.d.
John Suthiby of Burton to t. of Warter priory for all orders.
John son of John de Elmesale to t. of Selby abbey.
William Smyth of Hook to t. of Selby abbey for all orders.
John de Roclyff, to t. of St Andrew's priory, York, for all orders.
John Dalton to t. of St Oswald's priory, Nostell, for all orders.
Robert Halton to t. of Cartmel priory for all orders.
Thomas Hamylton to t. of the warden of the chantry of Sibthorpe.
John Barker to t. of Sinningthwaite priory for all orders.
Thomas Gemme to t. of Selby abbey.
Thomas Hall of Kneeton to t. of Newbo abbey for all orders.
Br. Elias Ward, O.F.M.
Br. Richard Gosberkyrk, O.F.M.
Br. John Malton, O.F.M.
Br. Thomas Byllyngsgate, O.F.M.
Br. Robert Hayton, O. Carm.
Br. Alan Wartr[e], O. Carm.
Br. John Feriby, O. Carm.
Br. Robert Hyldyrchelf, O.P.
Br. John Mellyng, O.P.
Br. John Mathirsey, canon of Mattersey.
Br. Thomas Wake, canon of Mattersey.
Br. William Pygot, monk of Fountains.
Br. William Tunstall, monk of Fountains.
Br. William Kyrkeby, O. Carth.
Br. Thomas Waplyngton, O. Carth.
Br. John de Tesdale, monk of St Mary's, York.
Br. Robert Toppeclyff, monk of St Mary's, York.

Priests

Thomas Norham, of Durham diocese, to t. of Alnwick abbey, by l.d.
John Bakster to t. of St Mary's hospital, Bootham, York.
Peter Moreby to t. of the cathedral church of York.
John de Whytby to t. of Wilberfoss priory.
John Austyn, of Carlisle diocese, to t. of William de Dacr[e], lord of Gilsland, by l.d.
William Spencer, of Durham diocese, to t. of Clementhorpe priory, by l.d.

folio

15v   Priests   cont.

John Altoftes to t. of St Oswald's priory, Nostell.
Richard Shadewell to t. of the collegiate church of Ripon for all orders.
William Bryggeford to t. of Shelford priory.
master Thomas Tesdale to t. of his church of St Crux, York.
Thomas Palmer of Long Buckby, of Lincoln diocese, to t. of Shelford Priory, by l.d.
John Layburn to t. of Clementhorpe priory.
Thomas son of Alan de Otryngham to t. of Swine priory.
Thomas Sutton to t. of St Mary's hospital, Bootham, York.
Thomas Roos to t. of Wilberfoss priory.
Robert Wryght to t. of St Andrew's priory, York.
John Brydlyngton to t. of Clementhorpe priory.
John Smyth of Normanton to t. of Shelford priory.
John Estwete to t. of Felley priory.
John Fyllyngham to t. of Shelford priory.
John Wryde to t. of Warter priory.
Simon Marflete to t. of the collegiate church of Beverley.
John Brown to t. of Wilberfoss priory.
Richard Pyrle to t. of Gokewell priory.
Richard Cotys to t. of Roche abbey.
Thomas 3ork to t. of Torksey priory.
William Fox to t. of Hampole priory.
Thomas Whyte to t. of Roche abbey.
Robert Pykburn to t. of Burton abbey.
John Boteler to t. of the collegiate church of Southwell.
Roger Brawby to t. of Selby abbey.
John Skelton to t. of St Leonard's hospital, York.
John Mop to t. of St Leonard's hospital, York.
William Fleshewer to t. of Arden priory.
Thomas Cotys, of Durham diocese, to t. of Swine priory, by l.d.

16   Br. John Benton, O.F.M.
Br. Walter Forman, O.F.M.
Br. John Graunt, O.F.M.
Br. Giles de Curia, O.F.M.
Br. John Belacys, O.F.M.
Br. Hugh de Harneham, monk of Meaux.
Br. John Torkesay, O.S.A.
Br. Robert Catton, canon of Bolton.
Br. William Ikelton, O. Carm.
Br. John Blaktoft, O. Carth.
Br. Robert Clapham, O.P.
Br. John Bro3irton, O.P.
Br. Robert Berwyk, monk of Fountains.
Br. William de Marton, monk of Rievaulx.

folio

16   Subdeacons - Rich(mond archdeaconry)

Br. Godwin de Melton, canon of Coverham.
Br. William de Hovyngham, monk of Calder, O. Cist.
Br. Richard del Thwayte, monk of Calder.
Br. Thomas de Hildyrwell, O.F.M.
Br. William Hoton, O.F.M.
Br. Simon Carlele, O.F.M.
Br. Michael Daunay, O.F.M.

Deacons

John de Warton to t. of Cockersand abbey for all orders.
John Martyll to t. of Sinningthwaite priory for all orders.
Richard Bennok to t. of Easby abbey for all orders.
Robert Mount to t. of Furness abbey for all orders.
Thomas Barton to t. of Neasham priory for all orders.
Br. Peter de Kendall, canon of Coverham.

ORDINATIONS CELEBRATED BY BR. RICHARD, EPISCOPUS SERVIENSIS AND SUFFRAGAN OF ARCHBISHOP WALDBY, IN THE COLLEGIATE CHURCH OF RIPON, ON 22 DECEMBER 1397.

Acolytes

William de Hexham.
William de Norton.
Roger Fraunk.
William de Roclyff.
William Kelm.

Thomas de Loncastr[e].
Roger de Tanfeld.
Br. John de Hoton, monk of Meaux.
Br. William de Naffreton,
   monk of Meaux.

Subdeacons

William de Midilton to t. of the collegiate church of Ripon.
William de Beswyk to t. of the collegiate church of Ripon.
Thomas Wyverthorp to t. of the collegiate church of Ripon.
Thomas Northows to t. of the collegiate church of Ripon.
Robert Dawtr[e] to t. of the cathedral church of York.
William Ode of Langar to t. of Newstead in Sherwood priory.
William Wryght of Dunnington to t. of St Mary's hospital,
   Bootham, York.
William Lax, of Durham diocese, by l.d., to t. of five marks
   from the income of William Morton of Darlington.
John de Cetyll to t. of Sawley abbey.
John Dodemore to t. of Meaux abbey.

47

folio

16   Subdeacons   cont.

John Crok to t. of Monk Bretton priory.
John Sowleby, of Carlisle diocese, by l.d., to t. of
    Clementhorpe priory.
Thomas Bolton of Hooton Pagnell to t. of Hampole priory.
John Gamyll, of Durham diocese, by l.d., to t. of St Mary's
    hospital, Bootham, York.
John son of John Smyth of Skellow to t. of Hampole priory.
John Esyngwald to t. of Nun Monkton priory.
John de Westwyk to t. of the collegiate church of Ripon.
John Holme to t. of St Mary's hospital, Bootham, York.
John Brootes of Otley to t. of Arthington priory.
John de Fryeston to t. of Swine priory.
John Gournes to t. of Arden priory.
John de Hoton to t. of Jervaulx abbey.
Thomas Nelson to t. of Malton priory.
John Coterell to t. of Beauchief abbey.
Richard Lusdall of Stubbs to t. of Clementhorpe priory.
Robert Gudall to t. of Warter priory.
William Lubyas to t. of the collegiate church of Howden.
Richard Gyliot to t. of Watton priory.
John Lawson to t. of Cockersand abbey.
Br. John Wyrcetr[e], canon of Malton.
Br. Richard Thorp, canon of Malton.
Br. John Holteby, canon of Malton.
Br. Robert de Wardall, canon of Malton.
Br. William de Skyren, monk of Meaux.
Br. William de Arnald, canon of Bridlington.

Deacons

Thomas Bellerby to t. of Coverham abbey.
Thomas de Burgh to t. of Easby abbey.
William Pathorn to t. of Warter priory.
William Lekynfeld to t. of Swine priory.
Richard Campsall to t. of Ulverscroft [Ulcroft] priory.
Thomas Eglysclyff, of Durham diocese, to t. of Neasham
    priory, by l.d.
Richard Bryg to t. of Newstead in Sherwood priory.
John Taylour of Tickhill to t. of Roche abbey.
Robert Smyth of Besthorpe to t. of Rufford abbey.
John Bolet to t. of Shelford priory.
John Palmer to t. of Rosedale priory.
Henry Graysothen to t. of Louth Park abbey.
Robert Catryk to t. of Keldholme priory.
Thomas Hall of Melton to t. of Clementhorpe priory.
William Halstede to t. of Sawley abbey.
William de Gresyngham to t. of Sawley abbey.

folio

16   Deacons   cont.

    John Aghen to t. of St Leonard's hospital, York.
    John Hughson to t. of Keldholme priory.
    Thomas Swanland to t. of the cathedral church of York.
    Br. Thomas Hildirwell, O.F.M. of Richmond.
    Br. William Boston, O. Carm. of York.
    Br. John Stepyng, O. Carm. of York.
    Br. Godwin Melton, canon of Coverham.

16v   Br. William Thyrntoft, O. Carm. of Doncaster.

    Priests

    Thomas Mauly to t. of Watton priory.
    Thomas Holme to t. of Clementhorpe priory.
    John Crayk to t. of Kepier hospital.
    Thomas Frawnkelayn to t. of Shelford priory.
    John Midelton to t. of the collegiate church of Ripon.
    Thomas Newham to t. of his church of Long Newton, Durham
        diocese.
    William Walker to t. of Kirkstall abbey.
    Robert Eglysclyff, of Durham diocese, to t. of Neasham
        priory, by l.d.
    Robert Halton, to t. of Cartmel priory.
    John Sproxton to t. of Moxby priory.
    Walter de Buttyrwyk to t. of Wykeham priory.
    John Barker to t. of Sinningthwaite priory.
    master Robert Camerton, of Carlisle diocese, to t. of
        patrimony, by l.d.
    John Marthill of Walton to t. of Sinningthwaite priory.
    Richard Gardyner, of Durham diocese, to t. of Egglestone
        abbey, by l.d.
    John de Dalton to t. of St Oswald's priory, Nostell.
    William de Cawode to t. of St Leonard's hospital, York.
    Henry de Illyngworth to t. of his church of Hatcliffe,
        Lincoln diocese.
    Robert Bothumsell to t. of Welbeck abbey.
    John Sotheby to t. of Warter priory.
    William Smyth of Hook to t. of Selby abbey.
    John Helmesale to t. of Selby abbey.
    John Daget to t. of Malton priory.
    John Roclyff to t. of St Andrew's priory, York.
    John Roklay to t. of St Andrew's priory, York.
    Thomas Barton to t. of Neasham priory.
    Richard Bennok to t. of Easby abbey.

folio

16v   Priests   cont.

        Robert Mount to t. of Furness abbey.
        Br. John Kyrkeby, monk of Pontefract.
        Br. William Lawton, monk of Pontefract.
        Br. Richard Devyas, monk of Pontefract.
        Br. William Marton, monk of Rievaulx.
        Br. Adam Swynshevyd, O. Carm. of York.
        Br. Alan Wartr[e], O. Carm.
        Br. Nicholas Midelton, O. Carm.

GENERAL INDEX

Personal names appear in the form in which they occur in the text, with cross-references from variant spellings. Where it has proved possible to identify territorial surnames, the modern equivalent has been added in round brackets. Obviously in most cases a positive identification could not be made: e.g. Calthorn is clearly the modern Cawthorne but it is impossible to ascertain whether Cawthorne in the West Riding of Yorkshire or Cawthorne in the North Riding is meant.

The following abbreviations have been used: abp – archbishop; bp – bishop; knt – knight; n – note.

abbeys, abbots
   see under names of individual religious houses
absence, leave of see licences for non-residence
absolution ad cautelam 4
acquittance of executors 12,17, 19,25
Acres, Thomas del 27
Addesun, Addisun, John 37,41
affinity
   see dispensation from impediment of affinity to marriage
Aghen, John [de] 44,49
Aglum, Richard, of Beverley 9
Aire, France, bishop of (Robert Waldby) ii
Alberwyk, Peter de, rector of Moor Monkton 6
Aldbrough
   chantry of St German 11
      chantry chaplain see Curtays, Robert
   parish church 11
   see also Fosham
Alexander, prior of Hexham see Marton, Br. Alexander de
alien priory, in the king's hands 35
Allerton, John de 39
   Thomas de 39
Almanbury (Almondbury), William 42
Alnwick, Nbld., abbey of 41,45
Alta Ripa, Robert de 43
   see also Dawtr[e]
altars, dedication, consecration and reconciliation 3
   suspension, if unconsecrated 3

Altoftes (Altofts), John 41,46
anniversaries 20
Appilton (Appleton), John, rector of Gilling in Rydale 12,19
   Robert de, rector of Huggate 12
archbishops
   see Canterbury
      Dublin
      York
archdeaconries
   see Cleveland
      Durham
      East Riding
      Nottingham
      Richmond
      York
Arden, prioress of 16
   priory of 16,46,48
Arnald, Br. William de, canon of Bridlington 48
Arthington, prioress of 30
   priory of 48
Arundel, Thomas, abp of York, then abp of Canterbury ii, iii,5,6
   register iv,9,10,12,22n
Askam, Askeham, Richard [de] 20; chaplain of the chantry of St Mary, Scarborough 21, 34; vicar of Scarborough 35
Askby, William de, rector of a mediety of Eakring 34
Askeham
   see Askam
Assburn, Robert, rector of St Peter the Little, York 36
Asselby, pa. Howden
   chapel 17

51

at Well
  see Well
Aton, William de, vicar of Kirkby
  in Cleveland 23
Attenborough, Notts.
  see also Chilwell
Aughton
  parish church 33
    custodian of see
      Hoveden, Br. Thomas de
Augustinian friars
  see Austin friars
Auncel, William 24
Austin friars see
  Blake, Br. Robert
  Duffelde, Br. Robert
  Torkesay, Br. John
  Yrchestr[e], Br. Thomas
Austyn, John 41,45
Axiholme (Axholme), Peter 12
Baglay, Br. Thomas, canon of
  Easby 42
Bainton
  rector of see Gudhall, Roger
  William Pynder of see Pynder
Bakster, John 41,45
  Thomas, of Rotherham 17
Bampton, John de 39
Banaster, Robert 43
Barker, John 38,45,49
  Robert 38
Barnbrough
  Thomas Parmeter of see Parmeter
Barnby, Barneby, Thomas, vicar of
  the prebend of Saltmarsh in
  Howden collegiate church 2
  Thomas [? another] 24
Barnoldswick
  see also Coates
        Walden
Barrowby
  John Harpeham of see Harpeham
Barry, Br. Thomas, O.Carm. of
  Doncaster 43,44
Barton, Thomas 40,47,49
bastardy
  see dispensations for bastardy
Baylers, Thomas 43
Beauchief, Derbys., abbey of 48
Beauvale, Notts., prior and convent
  of 29
Bedale
  John Hoton of see Hoton
Belacys, Br. John, O.F.M. 46
Belbyrby, Bellerby (Bellerby), Thomas
  40,48
benediction of ecclesiastical
  vestments and ornaments 3

benefice(s)
  see chantries
      collations
      custody
      exchanges
      institutions
      licences for farming
      mandates for induction
      prebends
      rectories
      vicarages
Benet, Robert 42
Bennok, Richard 40,47,49
Benton, Br. John, O.F.M. 46
Bernston [unidentified]
  Thomas Rose de see Rose
Berwyk, Br. Robert, monk of
  Fountains 46
Besthorpe, Notts.
  Robert son of Richard Smyth
  of see Smyth
Beswyk (Beswick), Richard 39
  William de 47
Beverlay (Beverley), John de
                  36
Beverley 17
  collegiate church of St
  John 38,39,40,41,42,43,46
    vicar in see Louthorp,
    Robert
  Richard Aglum of see Aglum
Bewyk (Bewick), John 39
Billyngham (Billingham),
  William de 42
Billysthorp (Bilsthorpe), Br.
  Simon, canon of Welbeck 40
bishops
  see Aire
      Chichester
      Durham
      Lincoln
      London
      Norwich
      Serviensis
      Whithorn
Blakburn (Blackburn)
  Br. John, monk of Whalley 40
  William 4
Blake, Br. Robert, O.S.A. of
  York 44
Blaktoft (Blacktoft), Br. John,
  O.Carth. 46
Bland, William 42
Blendale, Andrew 12
Blundell, master Robert,
  notary public 24
Bolet, John 48

Bolton
  canons of
    see Catton, Br. Robert
        Pleselay, Br. John
  Master Peter de, rector of
    Scrayingham 16
  Thomas, of Hooton Pagnell 48
  Thomas de, of Pontefract 43
  Br. William de, canon of
    Hexham 4
Boniface IX, Pope 5,21,28
  ambassador of see Nonatola
Bootham hospital
  see York, hospital of St Mary,
    Bootham
Bossall, church of 31
Boston, Br. William, O.Carm. of
  Doncaster and of York 44,49
Boteler, John 46
Bothumsell (Bothamsall), Robert 40,
  44,49
Botylstane, Br. Philip de 43
Bowet, Henry, abp of York
  register v
Braithwell 12
Brakken, William son of Peter
  de 40,44
Brammelay (Bramley), Br. Henry de,
  canon of Worksop, vicar of
  Sheffield 37
Brandsby, rectors of see
  Deen, John
  Middelton, John
  rectory of 6,7
Brantingham, church of 10
  see also Siggeston, master
    John de
Brawby, Roger 46
Braybrooke, Robert, bp of
  London 15
Bridlington, canon of see
  Arnald, Br. William de
  see also Brydlyngton
Broadholme, Notts., priory of 42
Broculstow (Broxstow), Lucy wife
  of Richard, of Edingley 29
Brootes, John, of Otley 48
Brott, Richard 37,42
Broughton, master Robert de,
  rector of Colkirk 24
Brown, John 41,46
  Robert 42
  Thomas 38,39
Broʒirton (Brotherton), Br. John,
  O.P. 46
Brydlyngton (Bridlington), John 46
  see also Bridlington

Bryg[g], Richard 43,48
Bryggeford (Bridgford),
  William 46
Brygham (Brigham), Elizabeth 7
  John 7
Brygman, Thomas 39
Buckby, Long, Northants.
  Thomas Palmer of see Palmer
Buckingham, John, bp of
  Lincoln 26
Bucton (Buckton), Robert de,
  chaplain of the chantry of
  St James, Scarborough 19
Buk, William 42
Bulmer, rural dean of 13,16
Burgh, Thomas de 48
Burnsall
  William son of Roger de
  Thorp of see Thorp
Burton
  John Suthiby of see Suthiby
Burton, Staffs., abbey of 46
Burton Agnes
  see Haisthorpe
Buttyrwyk (Butterwick),
  William de 49
Byland, abbot of see
  Pikeryng, master Geoffrey
  de
  monks of see
    Kylburn, Br. John
    Pykeryng, Br. John
    Sleford, Br. John
    Synington, Br. John
Byllyngsgate (Billingsgate),
  Br. Thomas,O.F.M. 45
Byrden, Br. John, O.Carm. of
  York 42
Byron, Sir Richard, knt 26
Calder, Cumbd., monks of see
  Hovyngham, Br.William [de]
  Rudstan, Br. Robert
  Skelton, Br. Thomas de
  Thwayte, Br. Richard del
Calthorn (Cawthorne), Robert 39
  see also Cawthorn
Camerton, master Robert 40,44,
  49
Campsale, Campsall, John de,
  vicar of Wadworth, rector
  of Leathley 13
  Richard [de] 43,48
Candida Casa
  see Whithorn
Canterbury, archbishop of, see
  Arundel, Thomas
  Convocation of the province
  of 32

Carboni, Francis, cardinal priest
    of St Susanna and papal
    penitentiary 5,26,27,35
cardinal
    see Carboni, Francis
Carlele (Carlisle), Br. Simon,
    O.F.M. 47
    see also Carlisle
Carleton, Br. Thomas de, canon of
    Newstead in Sherwood 44
    William, vicar-general of Bp
    Despenser of Norwich 2
    see also Carlton
Carlisle, diocese of 38,39,41,42,
    44,45,48,49
    see also Carlele
Carlow[e]
    see Karlow
Carlton by Snaith 17
    see also Carleton
Carmelite friars see
    Barry, Br. Thomas
    Boston, Br. William
    Byrden, Br. John
    Feriby, Br. John
    Hayton, Br. Robert
    Ikelton, Br. William
    Midilton, Br. Nicholas de
    Otteley, Br. John
    Skelton, Br. William
    Spowndon, Br. John
    Swynshevide, Br. Adam
    Thirletoft, Br. William
    Wartr[e], Br. Alan
    Worcestr[e], Br. John
    Wyghall, Br. Thomas
Carter, William, of Tawton 43
Carthusian monks see
    Blaktoft, Br. John
    Kyrkeby, Br. William de
    Waplyngton, Br. Thomas
Cartmel, Lancs., priory of 40,42,44,
    45,49
Castro Novo, Br. Peter de, O.Cist.,
    warden of the church of
    Scarborough 19
Cateryk, Catryk (Catterick),
    Robert 39,43,48
Catton, Br. Robert, canon of
    Bolton 46
Catwick
    John Smyth of see Smyth
Cave, William de 32
Cawode, Cawod (Cawood)
    John 12

Cawode, Cawod (Cawood)
    master William de, vicar-
    general of Abp Waldby
    passim
    seal of, as vicar-general
        37
    William [de] [?another]
    38,41,49
Cawood
    Emmota Raby of see Raby
Cawthorn (Cawthorne), John,
    rector of a mediety of
    High Hoyland 11
    see also Calthorn
Cetyll, John de 47
Chadburn, Br. John, O.P. of
    York 42
Chammbyrlan
    see Chawmbyrlayn
chantries
    admissions to 14,21,22,
    27,29,31,34,36
    duties and responsibilities
    of chaplain 20
    foundation and ordination
    19,20
    survey of King Edward VI
        20
chapel, licence for divine
    service in 17
Chaster, William, chaplain of
    Melton chapel, chaplain of
    the Fraternity of the
    Blessed Virgin Mary,
    Newark 22
chastity, vow of 6
Chawmbyrlayn, Chammbyrlan,
    Robert, of Seamer 39,45
Chichester, bishop of (Robert
    Waldby) ii
Chilwell, pa. Attenborough,
    Notts.
    Robert Martill of see
    Martill
Chillwell (Chilwell), William
        30
church
    see benefice
Cistercian monks see
    Castro Novo, Br. Peter de
    Theobald, Br.
Clapham, Br. Robert, O.P. 46
Claveryng, Sir John, knt,
    bailiff of the liberty of
    Hexham 5
Clement VI, Pope 5

Clementhorpe priory
   see York. priory of Clementhorpe
Clerk, Adam 4
   Adam [? another] 20
   John, de Wymton 42
Cleveland, archdeacon of
   official of 5,7,23
Cliffe 18
   see also Clyff
Clifton 10
   see also Clyfton
Clowcroft, John 42
Clowe, Br. Nicholas, monk of
   Sawley 41
Clyff, Richard 18
Clyfton (Clifton), Br. Benedict de,
   canon of Welbeck 41
   see also Clifton
Coates, pa. Barnoldswick 18
Cockersand, Lancs., abbey of 40,
   47,48
Colkirk, Norf., rector of
   see Broughton, master Robert de
collations of benefices 1,8,15,24,
   25,28,36
Colman, Henry 42
commission(s)
   for exchange of benefices 2,6
   13,15,23,26
   for Official of the spirituality
   of Hexham 1
   for penitentiaries 2,3,8
   for suffragan bishop 3
   for vicar-general of abp 1,8
   to absolve 4
   to administer goods 27
   to be present at Convocation as
   abp's representatives 21
   to carry out a visitation of
   religious house 6,16
   to receive purgation 11
   to receive resignation 25
   to receive vow of chastity and
   bestow the veil 6
   to summon Convocation 21
confessors
   see licences to choose a confessor
      penitentiaries
confirmation of adults and children 3
consanguinity
   see dispensations from
   impediment of consanguinity
   to marriage
consecration of altars, chapels,
   churches and churchyards 3
   of chalices and patens 3

Convocation
   adjournment of 32
   commission to be present at,
   as abp's representatives 21
   commission to summon 21
   see also Canterbury.
         Convocation of the
         province of; York.
         Convocation of the
         province of
Cooke, Robert, of Hexham 8
correction, canonical 15
Coteler, Robert 41
Coterell, John son of Ralph 32
   John [? the same] 39,48
Cotes
   see Cotys
Cottingham, rector of
   see Notyngham, John de
Cottingwith, East
   William Rycale of see
   Rycale
Cotys, Cotes, Richard 41,46
   Thomas 41,46
Cotys in Waldyng (? Coates and
   Walden, pa. Barnoldswick) 18
Coventry and Lichfield,
   diocese of 43,45
Coverham, abbey of 40,42,48
   canons of see
      Kendale, Br. Peter de
      Melton, Br. Godwin de
Cowldon, John 42
Craven, Robert 9
Crayk (Crayke), John 40,44,49
Croke, Crok, John 32
   John [? the same] 48
Crophill and Oxton, prebend of,
   in Southwell collegiate
   church 15,23,24
      prebendaries of see
      Danby, master John
      Warre, master Thomas la
      Weston, master Thomas de
Cum ex eo
   see dispensations in
   accordance with the
   constitution Cum ex eo
Cunstabyll, Edmund 39
curia, papal 4
Curia, Br. Giles de, O.F.M. 46
Curtays, Robert, chaplain of
   St German's chantry,
   Aldbrough 11
custody of benefices 33

55

Dacr[e], William de, lord of
    Gilsland 41,45
Daget,Dagett, John 41,49
Dalby, master Thomas de, archdeacon
    of Richmond 21
Dalton, John [de] 40,45,49
Danby, master John, prebendary of
    Crophill and Oxton [Southwell],
    prebendary of Twiford [London],
    prebendary of Darlington 15
    John de 36
Danyell, Robert son of William, of
    Nottingham 27
Darell, Marmaduke, of Sessay 14
Darlington, co.Durh.
    prebendaries of see
        Danby, master John
        Weston, master Thomas de
    William Morton of see Morton
Darnyngton (Darlington), John,
    parson in the cathedral church
    of York 3
Daunay, Br. Michael,O.F.M. 47
Dawtr[e],(Dawtry), Robert 47
    see also Alta Ripa
Daynale, Gocelin 35
dedication of altars, chapels,
    churches and churchyards 3
Deen, Den, John, rector of Brandsby,
    prebendary of Stanwick [Ripon]
    6,7,16
Dent [unidentified]
    John Holme de see Holme
Derby, Richard, archdeacon of
    Nottingham see Westderby
Despenser, Henry, bp of Norwich 2
    vicar-general of
    see Carleton, William
Devyas, Br. Richard, monk of
    Pontefract 41,50
dilapidations 12,13
dioceses see
    Carlisle
    Coventry and Lichfield
    Durham
    Glasgow
    Lincoln
    London
    Norwich
    Worcester
    York
dispensation(s)
    for bastardy 9,26,27,32,33
    for canonical irregularity 22
    for plurality 28
    from attendance at synods 14,31
    34,36

dispensation(s)
    from impediment of affinity/
    consanguinity to marriage
    5,13,28,35
    in accordance with the
    constitution Cum ex eo 1,
    8,31,33
    see also licence(s)
Dodemore, John 47
Dominican friars see
    Bro3irton, Br. John
    Chadburn, Br. John
    Clapham, Br. Robert
    Godeworth, Br. Henry
    Harum, Br. William [de]
    Hert, Br. Alan de
    Hyldyrchelf, Br. Robert
    Kexby, Br. William de
    Mellyng, Br. John
    Myrtford, Br. Thomas de
    Oliver, Br. Robert
    Rayly, Br. John
    Segesfeld, Br. Thomas de
Doncaster, Carmelite friars of
    see Barry, Br. Thomas
        Boston, Br. William
        Thirletoft, Br. William
Doun, William 5
Dowdale, William de 36
Drax
    Emmota Swynflet of see
    Swynflet
Dublin, Ireland, abp of
    (Robert Waldby) ii
    seal of 1n,6n,8n
Duffeld, Duffelde (Duffield)
    Robert, rector of Keighley
    36
    Br. Robert, O.S.A. of York
    42
Dunnington
    rectors of see
        Farman, William
        Wetewang, Richard [de]
    rectory of 5,13
    William Wryght of see Wryght
Durham
    archdeacon of see
        Weston, master Thomas de
    bishop of see
        Skirlaw, Walter
    diocese of 4,38,39,40,41,
    42,43,44,45,46,47,48,49
    prior of 31
    prior and convent of 23,29,
    30,42
Dysny, John 17

Eaglescliffe, co. Durh.
   William Gentylman of see Gentylman
   see also Eglysclyff
Eakring, Notts., mediety of the
   rectory of 34
      rector of see
         Askby, William de
Easby, abbey of 40,42,47,48,49
   canons of see
      Baglay, Br. Thomas
      Synnyngton, Br. John
East Riding, archdeacon of the
   see Feryby, master William de
   official of 14,31,34,35
Ebyrston (Ebberston), Br. Richard, monk
   of Kirkstall 42
Eckington, Derbys., mediety of the
   church of 37,38
   see also Ingilby, John
Edingley, Notts.
   Lucy wife of Richard Broculstow of
   see Broculstow
Edward VI, King 20n
Edwyn, Emery 19,20n
Egglestone, abbey of 40,44,49
Eglysclyff (Eaglescliffe), Robert 40,
   45,49
   Thomas 43,48
   see also Eaglescliffe
Ellerton on Spalding Moor
   canon of see Hoveden, Br. Thomas de
   prior and convent of 33
   priory of 38
Elmesale, Elmesall, Helmesale
   (Elmsall) John 40,44
   John son of John de, of
   Swinefleet 39,45,49
Elmham, South, Suff.
   document dated at 2
Eltham, Kent
   documents dated at 6,8,21
Ergum, Sir William, knt 17
Estryngton (Eastrington), Robert 40,44
Estwete, (Eastwood), John 41,46
Esyngton (Easington), Richard 32
Esyngwald, Esyngwalde, Esyngwolde
   (Easingwold), John 43
   John [?the same] 48
   Thomas 34
   Br. William de 43
Etton, Thomas de, rector of
   Huggate 12
exchange of benefices 1-2,6-7,13,14,
   15,22,23-24,26-27,30,34-35
excommunication 4,5,12,27
expenses of the papal ambassador 21

Farman, William, provost of
   Kirkby Overblow 3; rector
   of Dunnington 5,13
farming of benefices
   see licences for farming of
   benefices
Farmlaw, Br. Robert, monk of
   Whalley 40
Farnsfield, Notts.
   Helen wife of John
   Horncastell of see
      Horncastell
   Henry de Stabyll of see
      Stabyll
   John del Stabyll of see
      Stabyll
Fedyrstonhalgarth, William 4
Fedyrstonhalgh, Robert 4
Felixkirk
   see Ravensthorpe
Felley, Notts., priory of 41,
   46
Fenton
   Robert Wryght of see Wryght
Feriby, Feryby (Ferriby)
   Henry de 43
   Br. John, O. Carm 45
   master Nicholas de, canon of
   York 21
   Robert 39
   William de 22,29
   master William de,
   archdeacon of the East
   Riding 21
Ferriby, North, prior and
   convent of 18
Feryby
   see Feriby
Fieldplumpton, pa. Kirkham,
   Lancs. 16
Fillyngham, Fyllyngham
   (Fillingham) John 41,46
Fishlake, church of 31
   vicarage of 30
   vicars of see
      Gaynesburgh, Robert [de]
      Sherman, Peter
Flecher, William 38
Fleshewer, William 46
Fletwode (Fleetwood), John 16
Flynt, Richard 9
Forman, Br. Walter, O.F.M. 46
fornication 15
Fosham, pa. Aldbrough 17
Fountains, monks of see
   Berwyk, Br. Robert
   Pygot, Br. William
   Tunstall, Br. William

Fox, William 41,46
Francis, cardinal priest of St
    Susanna see Carboni
Franciscan friars see
    Belacys, Br. John
    Benton, Br. John
    Byllyngsgate, Br. Thomas
    Carlele, Br. Simon
    Curia, Br. Giles de
    Daunay, Br. Michael
    Forman, Br. Walter
    Gosberkyrk, Br. Richard
    Graunt, Br. John
    Haliden, Br. William
    Hesilden, Br. Robert
    Hildyrwell, Br. Thomas de
    Hoton, Br. William
    Malton, Br. John
    Ward, Br. Elias
    Wellys, Br. Robert
Fraunk, Roger 47
Frawnkelan, Frawnkelayn, Thomas
    39,45,49
Frer[e], Robert son of William 43
Freston, John, of Holderness 43
friars see
    Austin friars
    Carmelite friars
    Dominican friars
    Franciscan friars
Fryeston, John de [? same as
    Freston] 48
Frysnay (? Friskney), William 38
Furness, Lancs.
    abbey of 40,47,50
    monk of see Thwaythes, Br.
    Richard
Fyllyngham
    see Fillyngham
Fynmer, Adam 44
Fysshelak (Fishlake), John 36
    see also Fishlake
Galloway
    see Whithorn
Gamyll, John 48
    Thomas 39
Gardiner, Gardyner, Richard 40,
    44,49
Gardner, Richard 39
Gargrave, Laurence 43
    Br. Robert, monk of
    Sawley 41
Garton, John 12
Gaynesburgh (Gainsborough)
    John 40
    Robert [de], vicar of Fishlake,
    vicar of Maltby 30

Gaythill (Gate Hill), Thomas of
    Kirk Hammerton 38
Gedling, Notts., rector of a
    mediety of see Killum,
    master Robert de
Gemme, Thomas, of Haddlesey
    40,45
Gentylman, William, of
    Eaglescliffe 43
Gilling in Rydale
    rector of see
        Appilton, John
    rectory of 19
Gilsland, Cumbd., lord of
    see Dacr[e], William de
Gisburn in Craven, vicar of
    see Godfrey
Glasgow, diocese of 41
Glover, John son of Henry, vicar of
    Kirkby in Cleveland 23
Godeworth, Br. Henry, O.P. of York
                                44
Godfrey, vicar of Gisburn in
    Craven 11
Gokewell, Lincs., priory of 37,
    41,42,46
Gosberkyrk (Gosberton), Br.
    Richard, O.F.M. 45
Gosner, Br. John, canon of St
    Oswald, Nostell 42
Goteson, William 5
    wife of see
        Lange, Matilda
Gournes, John 48
Goushill, Gouxhill, Gowsell
    (Goxhill), John de, vicar
    of Scarborough 19,31,35 ;
    chaplain of the chantry of
    St Mary, Scarborough 34
Goxhill, chantry of St Mary
    in church of 31
    chantry chaplains of see
        Holmeton, Henry
        Thirnom, Robert
    rectors of see
        Selby, Robert
        Whatton, John
    rectory of 14
Graunt, Br. John, O.F.M. 46
Graysothen (Greysouthen),
    Henry 43,48
Greasley, Notts.
    vicarage of 29
    vicars of
        see Kendale, master Richard
            Tymersholt, Robert de
Grene, Adam de 32
    Nicholas, vicar of Rothwell 12

58

Gressyngham, Gresyngham
    (Gressingham), William de 43,48
    see also Gryssyngham
Grey, John, lord of Sandiacre 26
Grindal, prebend of, in York
    Minster 23,24
    prebendaries of
        see Warre, master Thomas la
            Weston, master Thomas de
Grome, Robert 42
Grysmer, John 42
Gryssyngham (Gressingham), John 42
Gudall, Gudhall
    Robert 48
    Roger, rector of Bainton 11,12
Guisborough, canon of
    see Stafford, Br.John
    priory of 33
Gunnays, Thomas 12
Gyliot, Richard 48
Hackford, Norf., rectors of
    see Popilton, Adam de
        Quik, Rowland
Haddlesey
    Thomas Gemme of see Gemme
Haisthorpe, pa. Burton Agnes 10
Haliden (?Halidon), Br.William,
    O.F.M. of Richmond 41
Hall, Halle
    Robert de 4
    Robert, of Kneeton 39
    Thomas, of Kneeton 45
        (the above are probably
        identical, the change of
        Christian name being due
        to a scribal error)
    Thomas, of Melton 43,48
Haloughton
    see Halton
Halsted, Halstede (Halstead)
    William [de] 39,43,48
Halton, Haloughton, John, chaplain
    of the Fraternity of the Blessed
    Virgin Mary, Newark, chaplain of
    Melton chantry 22,29
    Robert [de] 40,45,49
Hamerton (Hammerton), Alan de 36
Hamlake, lord of
    see Roos, William de
    see also Helmsley
Hampole, priory of 38,41,43,46,48
Hamylton, Thomas 45
Hardegyll, John 42
Harneham (Harnham), Br. Hugh de,
    monk of Meaux 46
Harpeham (Harpham), John, of
    Barrowby 43

Harthill, rectors of
    see Spryngot, John
        Sutton, Elias [de]
Harum (Harome), Br. William
    [de] 39,40
Harwode (Harewood), John 12
    Richard de 40,45
Hasard, John 42
Hastinges, Sir Ralph de, knt 34
Hatcliffe, Lincs., church of 49
    see also Illyngworth, Henry
        [de]
Hawton, Notts., church of 43
    see also Baylers, Thomas
Hayhard, John 2
Hayton, Br. Robert, O.Carm. 45
Healaugh Park, prior and
    convent of 13
    priory of 42
Hedon, John 42
Hedryngton, Robert 4
Helmesale
    see Elmesale
Helmsley
    John Hughson of see Hughson
    see also Hamlake
Hemeswell (Hemswell), Br.
    Richard, canon of Hexham 15
Hemingbrough, parochial
    chaplain of see Stevynson,
    Roger
    see also Turnham Hall
Hemyngburgh (Hemingbrough),
    Robert, vicar of Skipwith 23
Hert, Br. Alan de, O.P. of
    York 44
Hesilden (Hesleden), Br. Robert,
    O.F.M. of Richmond 41
Heton, John, of Steeton 9
Heton [unidentified]
    John Man de see Man
Hexham, Nbld.
    liberty of
        Bailiff of see Claveryng,
        Sir John
        chancellor of abp in see
        Marton, Br.Alexander de
        tenant of see Stubbys,
        William
    peculiar jurisdiction of 1,2
        clergy of 2
        Official of see
        Laundelles, master Thomas
    priory of 6,15
        canons of
            see Bolton, Br.William
            de

59

Hexham, priory of (cont.)
   canons of
      see Hemeswell, Br.Richard de
         Wodhorn, Br.William
   prior of 6
      see also Marton, Br. Alexander
         de
   Robert Cooke of see Cooke
   William de 47
Hickling, Notts.
   rectors of see
      Wayte, John
      Wilford, Thomas
   rectory of 26,27
High Hoyland
   see Hoyland, High
Hildirwell, Hildyrwell
   (Hinderwell), Br.Thomas de, O.F.M.
   of Richmond 47,49
Hilton, Alan de 37,41
   Sir Robert, knt 9
Hockerton, Notts., rector of
   see Revell, master Thomas
Holderness
   John Freston of see Freston
Holm, Holme
   John 48
   John, de Dent 39
   Thomas 41,49
Holmcultram, Cumbd., abbey of 39
Holme
   see Holm
Holmeton (Holmpton), Henry, chaplain
   of St Mary's chantry, Goxhill 31
Holmpton
   see Rysome
Holteby, (Holtby), Br. John, canon
   of Malton 48
Holy Trinity priory, Micklegate see
   York. priory of Holy Trinity,
   Micklegate
Hook
   William Smyth of see Smyth
Hooton Pagnell
   Thomas Bolton of see Bolton
Horncastell (Horncastle), Helen
   wife of John, of Farnsfield 22
Hornsea, rectory house at 10
Hoton, John 9
   John 39,48
   John, of Bedale 43
   Br. John de, monk of Meaux 47
   Br. William, O.F.M. 47
Hoveden (Howden), Br. Thomas de,
   canon of Ellerton, custodian
   of Aughton church 33

Hovyngham (Hovingham), Br.
   William [de], monk of Calder
   43,44,47
Howby, John, chaplain of St
   Mary's chantry, Sibthorpe 14
Howden
   collegiate church of 2,48
   prebends in
      see Howden
         Saltmarsh
   prebendal vicar of
      see Barneby, Thomas
   prebend of 29
   prebendaries of
      see Sergeaux, master
         Michael
         Strykland, William de
   see also Asselby
        Hoveden
Howdenshire
   peculiar jurisdiction of
   custodian of the
      spirituality of 22,23,29
   penitentiary in
      see Barneby, Thomas
Hoyland, High, rector of a
   mediety of see Cawthorn, John
Huggate, rectors of
   see Appilton, Robert de
      Etton, Thomas de
Hughson, John, of Helmsley 43,49
   see also Huson
Hull, Carthusian monks of
   see Kyrkeby, Br. William de
      Waplyngton, Br. Thomas
Huson, John [? same as Hughson]
   39
Hyldyrchelf (Hinderskelfe),
   Br. Robert, O.P. 45
Hyll, Robert de 17
Ikelton (Hickleton), Br.
   William, O. Carm. 46
Illyngworth, Yllyngworth
   (Illingworth), Henry
   [de] 39,44,49
income of the archdeaconry of
   Nottingham 27
induction
   see mandates for induction
Ingilby, Ingylby, John 3,37,38
injunctions
   see visitation
institutions
   by reason of exchanges
      see exchanges

institutions (cont.)
   to benefices 2,3,5,6,7,13,14,22,
     23,26,27,28,29,30,31,34,35,36,37
Ipre, Sir Ralph de, knt 6,15
   Emmota, widow of 6,15
irregularity, canonical 22
Ivun, John 44
Jervaulx, abbey of 48
Jervous, Henry 41
Jors, Robert 42
Karlow, Carlow[e], Br. Thomas, monk
   of Pontefract 22 & n, 41
Keighley, rector of
   see Duffeld, Robert
Keldholme, priory of 43,48,49
Keleby, Br. John, monk of Whalley 40
Kellow (Kelloe), Thomas, rector of
   Lythe 31
Kelm, William 47
Kembe, Keme, Robert 37,42
Kendale, Kendall (Kendal)
   Br. Peter de, canon of
     Coverham 40,47
   Master Richard, vicar of
     Greasley 29
Kepier, co. Durh., hospital of 39,49
Keworth (Keyworth), William, chaplain
   of Melton chantry 29
Kexby, Br. William de, O.P. 40
Killingwoldgraves, hospital of 43
Killom, Killum, Kyllum (Kilham)
   master Richard de, rector of
     a mediety of Gedling 14
   Thomas 38,42
Kilner, Christine 35
Kings
   see Edward VI
     Richard II
Kingston upon Hull
   see Hull
Kirby cum Broughton
   see Kirkby in Cleveland
Kirk Hammerton
   Thomas Gaythill of see Gaythill
Kirkandris (Kirk Andrews), John 39
Kirkby in Cleveland
   vicarage of 23
   vicars of
     see Aton, William de
       Glover, John son of Henry
Kirkby Overblow, provosts of
   see Farman, William
     Whitewell, John
   provostship of 3
Kirkham, Lancs.
   see Fieldplumpton
Kirklees, priory of 43

Kirkstall, abbey of **40,44,49**
   monk of
     see Ebyrston, Br. Richard
Knayton, Robert 43
Kneeton, Notts.
   Robert Hall of see Hall
   Thomas Hall of see Hall
Knolles, Sir Robert, knt 27,28
Kylburn (Kilburn), Br. John,
   monk of Byland 40
Kyllum
   see Killom
Kyndenesse, John, rector of
   Warmsworth 35
Kyrkeby (Kirkby)
   Br. John, monk of Pontefract
     50
   Br. William [de], O. Carth
     of Hull 40,45
Kyrketon, Thomas, rector of
   Terrington 34
Lafford, Sleforde, prebendary
   of, in Lincoln cathedral
   see Warre, master Thomas la
Laghton (Laughton), master
   Robert 37
Landmoth, pa. Leake 11
Langar, Notts.
   William Ode of see Ode
Lange, Matilda, wife of
   William Goteson 5
Lasyng, John 39
Laundelles, master Thomas,
   Official of Hexham 1
Laverok (Laverack), Robert 40
Lawson, John 48
Lawton, Br. William, monk of
   Pontefract 50
Lax, William 47
Layburn (Leyburn), John 41,46
   William 34
Leake
   see also Landmoth
Leathley, rectors of
   see Campsale, John de
     Maundeville, William
   rectory of 13
Ledys (Leeds), Simon 42
Leicester, abbey of Delapré, 42
Lekynfeld (Leconfield), William
   43,48
Leley (Lelley), Ralph 14
letters dimissory 1,3,4,5,8,9,
   18,26,32,33,34,36
   of collation
     see collations

letters (cont.)
  of institution
    see institutions
  testimonial of ordination 9,10,12
Lewes, Sussex, prior and convent of 35
licence(s)
  for divine service in a chapel 17
  for farming of benefices 10,12,13,
  14,16,19,30,31,34,36
  for non-residence
    for fear of death 11
    for one year 13,14,16,30,36
    for two years 19,31
    for three years 34
  for private oratories 1,7,8,9,10,
  11,12,14,15,16,17,18
  to celebrate private masses for
  the living and the dead 11
  to choose a confessor 10
  see also dispensations
Lincoln
  bishop of
    see Buckingham, John
  cathedral church of
    prebendary of
      see Warre, master Thomas la
  diocese of 24,38,40,46,49
Loncastr[e] (Lancaster), Thomas
  de 47
London
  bishop of
    see Braybrooke, Robert
  cathedral church of St Paul's
    prebend of
      see Twiford
    prebendaries of
      see Danby, master John
          Weston, master Thomas
          de
  documents dated at 1,15,21,23,
  31,33
Long Buckby
  see Buckby, Long
Long Newton
  see Newton, Long
Louth Park, Lincs., abbey of 43,48
Louthorp (Lowthorpe), Robert, vicar
  in Beverley collegiate church 3
Lubyas, William 48
Lunde (Lund), John 38
  William 39
Lusdall, Richard, of Stubbs 48
Lyndale, John de 12
Lythe, rector of
  see Kellow, Thomas
Maltby, vicarage of 30

Maltby (cont.)
  vicars of
    see Gaynesburgh,
        Robert [de]
      Sherman, Peter
Malton, priory of 41,48,49
  canons of
    see Holteby, Br.John
      Thorp, Br.Richard
      Wardall, Br.Robert
      de
      Wyrcetr[e],Br.John
  Br. John, O.F.M. 45
  Richard, rector of
  Thornton Dale 10
Man, John, de Heton 39
Manchestr[e] (Manchester),
  Thomas, citizen of York 12
mandate(s) for induction 1,3,
  5,6,7,13,14,21,22,23,27,28,
  29,30,31,34,35,36,37
  for installation 15,24,
  25,28
  to enjoin penance 4
  to enquire about non-
  residence 16
  to obey new archdeacon 26
  to relax sequestration 13
Manneby (Manby), Thomas 38
Mannely, Thomas [?same as
  Manneby] 42
Marchall
  see Marshall
Marflete (Marfleet), Simon
  41,46
Market Weighton
  see Weighton, Market
Markham, John 15
Marshall, Marchall
  John 38
  John 43
  Robert 42
  William, of Tadcaster 39
Martill, Marthill, Martyll
  John,of Walton 40,47,49
  Robert,of Chilwell 30
    Agnes, wife of 30
Marton, Br. Alexander de,
  prior of Hexham 4,5
  Br. William de, monk of
  Rievaulx 46,50
Martyll
  see Martill
Martynson, Thomas 39
Masbrough, pa. Rotherham 31
Mason
  see Masun

masses, private 11
Masun, Mason
   John, of Poppleton, rector
     of Moor Monkton 6,42
   John 37
   William 20
Mathirsey (Mattersey), Br.John,
   canon of Mattersey 45
Mattersey, Notts.
   priory of 42
      canons of see
         Mathirsey, Br.John
         Wake, Br. Thomas
Maukyn, Stephen 42
Maulay, Mauly, Thomas 41,49
Maundeville, Maundevyle, William,
   rector of Leathley, vicar of
   Wadworth 13
Mayre, William 40
Meaux, abbey of 42,47
   monks of see
      Harneham, Br. Hugh de
      Hoton, Br. John de
      Naffreton, Br. William de
      Skyren, Br. William de
Meldy, William 38
Mellyng, (Melling), Br. John,
   O.P. 45
Melton
   Thomas Hall of see Hall
   Br. Godwin [de], canon of
     Coverham 47,49
   William, abp of York i
Melton, pa. Welton
   chantry in chapel of 22,29
      chaplains of see
         Chaster, William
         Halton, John
         Keworth, William
Merley, William 4
Middelton, Midelton, Midilton,
   Mydelton (Middleton)
   John de 39
   John [de] 39,44,49
   John, prebendary of Stanwick
     [Ripon], rector of Brandsby 6
   Br. Nicholas de, O.Carm. 38,50
   William de 47
Midelham (Middleham), John, of
   York 43
Midelton
   see Middelton
Midilton
   see Middelton
Milner, Edwin 20n
   Emery 20n
   Reginald 19,20n

monasteries
   see religious houses
Monk Bretton, priory of 48
monks
   see under names of
   individual religious houses
Moor Monkton
   rectors of see
     Alberwyk, Peter de
     Masun, John, of Poppleton
   rectory of 6,42
Mop, Mopp, John 41,46
Moreby, Peter 45
Morton, William, of Darlington
     47
Mount, Mounte, Robert 40,47,50
Moxby, priory of 40,44,49
muniments of the abp in
   Hexhamshire 2,5
Mustardmaker, Alice, of Ripon
     19
Mydelton
   see Middelton
Myrtford, Br. Thomas de, O.P.
   of York 44
Naffreton (Nafferton), Br.
   William de, monk of
   Meaux 47
Naylston (Nailstone), Henry 10
Neasham, co. Durh., priory
   of 40,43,45,47,48,49
Nelson, Thomas 48
Nettleham, Lincs.
   document dated at 26
Neuton
   see Newton
Neville, Alexander, abp of
   York iii
Newark, Notts.
   parish church of St Mary
   Magdalen 22
     chantry of the
     Fraternity of the
     Blessed Virgin Mary at
     the altar of All Saints
     in 22
       chaplains of see
         Chaster, William
         Halton, John
       warden of see
         Seynell, Richard
     master Alan 21
Newbo, Lincs., abbey of 39,45
Newby, Robert de 19
Newcastle, Nbld., Franciscan
   friar of see Wellys, Br.
     Robert
   see also Novo Castro

Newham, Thomas 44,49
Newstead in Sherwood, Notts.
    priory of 43,47,48
        canon of see
            Carleton, Br.Thomas de
Newton, Neuton
    master John de, treasurer of
    York 21
    William de, prebendary of the
    chapel of St Mary and the
    Holy Angels, York 36
Newton, Long, co.Durh., church
    of 44,49
    see also Newham, Thomas
non-residence 16
    see also licences for
    non-residence
Nonantola, Italy, abbot of 21
Norham, Thomas 41,45
Normanton
    John Smyth of see Smyth
North Ferriby
    see Ferriby, North
Northows, Thomas 47
Northumberland, earl of
    see Percy, Henry [de]
Northwell (Norwell), Br.William
    de, canon of Shelford 42
Norton, William de 47
    master William, rector of
    Tanfield 31
Norwich, bishop of
    see Despenser, Henry
    diocese of 1,24
Nostell, priory of St Oswald 38,
    40,41,42,44,45,46,49
        canons of see
            Gosner, Br. John
            Orberye, Br. William de
notary public
    see Blundell, master Robert
Notbroun, Gilbert, chaplain
    of St Mary's chantry,
    Sibthorpe 14
Notingham
    see Notyngham
Nottingham, archdeacon of
    see Notyngham, John de
        Westderby, Richard
    official of 14,22,27,29,34
    archdeaconry of 3,25,27,28
        annual income of 27
        clergy and people of 26
    Robert son of William Danyell
    of see Danyell
    wife [unnamed] of Robert
    Squier of see Squier
    John Wryght of see Wryght

Notyngham, Notingham
    (Nottingham)
    John de, rector of
    Cottingham, archdeacon
    of Nottingham 25,26,27,28
Nun Monkton, priory of 38,48
nuns, seducers of 8
obits 20
Ode, William, of Langar 47
Oliver, Br. Robert, O.P.
    of York 43,44
oratories
    see licences for private
    oratories
Orberye, Br. William de,
    canon of St Oswald,
    Nostell 42
ordinations 3,22n,37-50
    see also letters dimissory,
    letters testimonial of
    ordination
Ormesby, John de 39
    Peter 38
ornaments, benediction of
    ecclesiastical 3
Oswald, Br., bp of Whithorn
    and suffragan of abp
    Waldby ii,iii,3,10,12,
    37,38,39,43
Otlay
    see Otteley
Otley, rural dean of 13
    John Brootes of see Brootes
Otryngham (Ottringham)
    Thomas son of Alan de 46
Otryngton (Otterington)
    Br. Robert, monk of
    Whalley 40
Otteley, Otlay (Otley)
    Br. John, O.Carm. of
    Doncaster 39,44
Oudeby, master Ralph 6
Oxton, William de 26
Oxton Prima Pars, prebend of
    see Crophill and Oxton
Padlay, Richard, chaplain
    of St Mary's chantry,
    Sibthorpe 14
Palmer, John 43,48
    Thomas, of Long Buckby 46
papal curia 4
papal penitentiary 13
    see also Carboni, Francis
parks of the abp, those
    breaking into the 8

Parlyngton (Parlington)
    John, chaplain of a chantry
    in Holy Trinity college,
    Pontefract 28
Parmeter, Thomas, of Barnbrough 39,43
Pathorn (Paythorne)
    William [de] 43,48
Patson, Adam, of Weighton 43
peculiar jurisdictions
    see Hexham
        Howdenshire
penance 4,15
penitentiaries 2,3,8
    see also papal penitentiary
pension provided for the retiring
    archdeacon of Nottingham 27
Pepircorn, Henry, chaplain of St
    Mary's chantry, Sibthorpe 14
Percy, Henry [de], earl of
    Northumberland 3,5
permutations
    see exchanges
Pikeryng, Pykeryng (Pickering)
    master Geoffrey de, abbot of
    Byland 16
    Br. John, monk of Byland 40
Pleselay (Pleasley)
    Br. John, canon of Bolton 42
Pokethorp (Pockthorpe) John 10
Polles, Henry 38,39
Pontefract
    priory of 22
        monks of see
            Devyas, Br. Richard
            Karlow, Br. Thomas
            Kyrkeby, Br. John
            Lawton, Br. William
        Thomas de Bolton of see Bolton
Popes
    see Boniface IX
          Clement VI
Popilton (Poppleton)
    Adam de, rector of Hackford,
    rector of Thornton in Craven
    1,2
    John de, vicar choral of York
    Minster 36
    Thomas, prebendary of the chapel
    of St Mary and the Holy Angels 36
Poppleton
    John Masun of see Masun
Porter, John 39
prebends, admissions to 6,7,15,
    23-24,29,36
Preston, Thomas 44
priories
    see alien priory

priories (cont.)
    and also under names of
    individual religious houses
priors
    see under names of
    individual religious houses
private masses
    see licences to celebrate
    private masses for the
    living and the dead
private oratories
    see licences for private
    oratories
probate
    see wills
proctors 2,24,27,29,37
procurations, collection of 3
protestation, solemn 24,28
provostship of Kirkby
    Overblow 3
purgation 11
Pygot, Br. William, monk of
    Fountains 45
Pykburn (Pickburn), Robert 46
Pykeryng see Pikeryng
Pykton (Picton)
    John de, chaplain of the
    chantry at the altar of
    St John the Baptist in the
    church of St Peter the
    Little, York 36
Pynder, William, of Bainton 11
    Idonea, widow of 11,12
Pyrle, Richard 41,46
Quik, Qwhyk, Rowland, rector of
    Thornton in Craven, rector
    of Hackford 1,2
Quynton (Quinton), John 37,39
Qwhyk
    see Quik
Raby, Emmota, of Cawood 33
Raper, Robert 42
Rasyn, master Richard 25
Ravensthorpe 18
Ravynthorp (Ravensthorpe)
    Thomas 18
Rayly, Br. John, O.P. of York 42
reconciliation of altars,
    chapels, churches and
    churchyards 3
rectories, admissions to 1,5,
    6,10,13,14,26-27,34,35
Rednes (Reedness), John 12,24
registers of the abps of York
    iii-v,9,10,12,22n,37
religious houses, visitation
    of 6,16

religious houses (cont.)
   and see under names of
   individual religious houses
Rembon, Thomas 39
resignation of the archdeacon of
   Nottingham 25
Retteford (Retford), John de 17
Revell, master Thomas, rector of
   Hockerton 30
Richard, Br. episcopus Serviensis,
   suffragan of Abp Waldby ii,iii,
   9,47
   II, King of England ii,19,21,35
Richemund (Richmond)
   John de, of Ripon 7
Richmond
   archdeacon of see
      Dalby, master Thomas de
   archdeaconry of 3
      penitentiary in see
         Darnyngton, John
      Franciscan friars of see
         Haliden, Br. William
         Hesilden, Br. Robert
         Hildirwell, Br. Thomas
Rievaulx, monk of see
   Marton, Br. William de
Ripon
   collegiate church of St Peter
   and St Wilfrid 37,38,39,41,42,
   44,46,47,48,49
      canon of see
         Cawode, master William de
      chapter of 7
      prebend of see
         Stanwick
      documents dated at 1,2,3,4,5,6,
      7,15,16,19,30,31,36,37
      Alice Mustardmaker of see
         Mustardmaker
      John Richemund of see
         Richemund
      Alice wife of Robert Skynner
      of see Skynner
Risum (Rysome), William 10
   see also Rysome
Rithir (Ryther), John de 19
Robynson, Thomas 38
Roche, abbey of 41,43,46,48
Roclyff, Rowclyff
   John [de] 40,45,49
   Sir Richard de, knt 18
      Margaret widow of 18
   William de 47
Rokhop, John de 4
Roklay (Rockley), John 41,49
Rome, Italy 5

Roos, Rose, Rosse
   Beatrice, lady de 1,2
   Thomas, de Bernston 41,46
   William de, lord of
      Hamlake 34
Rosedale, priory of 43,48
Rosse
   see Roos
Roston
   see Ruston
Roth, Sir Thomas, knt 18
Rotherham
   parish church of 31
   Thomas Bakster of see
      Bakster
   see also Masbrough
Rothwell, vicar of see
   Grene, Nicholas
Routh, William 39
Rowclyff
   see Roclyff
Rowsyde, John 4
Ruddington, Notts.
   church of 31
Rudstan (Rudston)
   Br. Robert, monk of Calder
      44
Rufford, Notts., abbey of
   43,48
   abbot of 31
Ruston, Roston
   Henry de 20
      Margery wife of 20
Rycale (Riccall)
   William, of East
      Cottingwith 13
Rysome, pa. Holmpton 10
   see also Risum
Rysselay (?Risley),
   Br. Thomas, monk of
      Whalley 40
Ryvere, Marmaduke de la 7
St Andrew's priory, York see
   York. priory of St Andrew
St Leonard's hospital, York
   see York. hospital of St
   Leonard
St Mary's hospital, Bootham
   see York. hospital of St
   Mary, Bootham
St Peter's, Rome 5
St Quintin, master Anthony
   of 10
St Susanna, cardinal priest
   of see Carboni, Francis

St Thomas' hospital outside
   Micklegate Bar see York.
   hospital of St Thomas outside
   Micklegate Bar
Salflet (Saltfleet)
   William 39
Saltmarsh, prebend of, in Howden
   collegiate church
     vicar of see Barneby, Thomas
Sandiacre, lord of
   see Grey, John
Sawley,
   abbey of 39,43,44,47,48
     monks of see
        Clowe, Br. Nicholas
        Gargrave, Br. Robert
Scarborough
   bailiffs and commonalty of 19,21,34
   church of St Mary
     alien priory of 35
       warden of see Castro Novo,
       Br. Peter de
     chantry of St James in
       chaplain of see Bucton, Robert
         de
     chantry of St Mary in 19-20,21
       chaplains of see Askam, Richard
          Goushill, John
   common hall at 19
   vicarage of 35
   vicars of see Askam, Richard
         Goushill, John
Scawceby (Scausby)
   Thomas de 29
Scrayingham, rector of see
   Bolton, master Peter de
Scrope, Richard, abp of York iii
   register v,22n
seal of Abp Waldby as abp of
   Dublin 1n,6n,8n
   of Abp Waldby as abp of York 15n
   of abp's vicar-general 37
Seamer
   Robert Chawmbyrlayn of see
   Chawmbyrlayn
sede vacante 2,20
Segefeld, Segesfeld (Sedgefield)
   John, rector of Stokesley 13
   Br. Thomas de, O.P. of York 44
Selby, abbey of 39,40,44,45,46,49
   Robert, rector of Goxhill, warden
    of St Mary's chantry, Sibthorpe 14
Sellestorn (Sigglesthorne)
   Br. Thomas 44
Selow, Roger 39
sequestration 13
Sergeaux, master Michael, prebendary
   of Howden 29

Serviensis episcopus
   see Richard, Br.
Sessay
   Marmaduke Darell of see
   Darell
Seton, Hugh 8
Seynell, Richard, warden of the
   Fraternity of the Blessed
   Virgin Mary, Newark 22
Shadewell (Shadwell)
   Richard 46
Shalford, Br. John de, canon
   of Watton 42
Sheffelde (Sheffield)
   Nicholas 11
   Thomas 12
Sheffield
   vicarage of 37
   vicars of see
     Brammelay, Br. Henry de
     Upton, Br. Roger de
Shelford, Notts.
   priory of 39,41,45,46,48,49
     canon of see
       Northwell, Br.William
         de
Sherburn, co. Durh.
   hospital of 38,42
Sherman, Peter, vicar of
   Maltby, vicar of Fishlake 30
Sibthorpe, Notts.
   chantry of St Mary 14
     chaplains of see
       Howby, John
       Notbroun, Gilbert
       Padlay, Richard
       Pepircorn, Henry
     wardens of 45
       see also
       Selby, Robert
       Whatton, John
Siggeston (Sigston)
   master John de, rector of
   Brantingham 10
Sinningthwaite, priory of 38,
   40,45,47,49
Skellow
   John, son of John Smyth of
   see Smyth
Skelton
   Br. Gerard, monk of
   Whalley 40
   John 41,46
   Br. Thomas de, monk of
   Calder 44
   Br. William [de], O.Carm.
   37,41

Skipwith
   vicar of see Hemyngburgh, Robert
   vicarage of 23
Skirlaw, Walter, bp of Durham 15
Skynner, Alice wife of Robert, of
   Ripon 19
Skyren (Skerne)
   Br. William de, monk of Meaux 48
Sleford (Sleaford), Br. John,
   monk of Byland 40
Sleforde (Sleaford, Lincs.)
   see Lafford
Smyth
   John, of Catwick 39
   John, of Normanton 41,46
   John son of John, of Skellow 48
   Robert son of Richard, of
   Besthorpe 43,48
   William, of Hook 39,45,49
Snoll, Robert 43
Sotheby
   see Suthiby
South Elmham
   see Elmham, South
Southwell, Notts.
   collegiate church of 41,44,46
      chapter of 15,24
      prebend of see Crophill and
      Oxton
      prebendaries of see
         Danby, master John
         Warre, master Thomas la
         Weston, master Thomas de
   documents dated at 22,23,24,25,
   26,27,28,29,30
   house of vicar-general at 24
   see also Suthwell
Sowleby, John 39,48
Sparowe, Robert, parson in the
   cathedral church of York 2
Spencer, William 37,45
Spicer, Spycer
   John 40,44
   William, chaplain of a chantry
   in Holy Trinity college,
   Pontefract 27
Spowndon, Br. John, O.Carm. 38
Sproxton, John 40,44,49
Spryngot, John, rector of
   Harthill 35
Spycer
   see Spicer
Squier, wife [unnamed] of Robert,
   of Nottingham 23
Stabyll
   Henry de, of Farnsfield 23
   John del, of Farnsfield 30
   William del 42

Stafford, Br. John, canon
   of Guisborough 33
Stanhope, co.Durh.
   parochial chaplain of 4
   rector of 4
Stanwick
   prebend of, in Ripon
   collegiate church 6,7
   prebendaries of see
      Deen, John
      Middelton, John
Stapilton, Miles de 17
   Thomas 28
Steeton
   John Heton of see Heton
Stepyng (Steeping)
   Br. John, O.Carm. of
   York 49
Stevynson, Roger, parochial
   chaplain of Hemingbrough 2
Stokesley, rector of
   see Segefeld, John
Strech, John 24
Stretton, John, chaplain of
   a chantry in Holy Trinity
   college, Pontefract 28
Strykland (Strickland)
   William de, prebendary
   of Howden 29
Stubbs
   Richard Lusdall of see
   Lusdall
Stubbys, William 4
suffragan bishops
   see Oswald, Br., bp of
   Whithorn
   Richard, Br., episcopus
   Serviensis
suspension of altars, if
   unconsecrated 3
Suthiby, Sotheby, John, of
   Burton 40,45,49
Suthwell (Southwell), master
   John de 6
   see also Southwell
Sutton
   Elias [de], rector of
   Harthill 25,35
   Thomas 38,41,46
   Br. Thomas de 43
Swanland, Thomas 43,49
Swine, priory of 38,40,41,
   43,46,48
Swinefleet
   John son of John de
   Elmesale of see Elmesale
   see also Swynflet

Swyneshede, Swynshevide, Swynshevyd (Swineshead)
   Br. Adam, O.Carm. of York 37,41,50
Swynflet (Swinefleet)
   Emmota, of Drax 7
Synington, Synnyngton (Sinnington)
   Br. John, monk of Byland 40
   Br. John, canon of Easby 42
synods 14,31,34,36
   see also Convocation
Tadcaster
   William Marshall of see Marshall
Tadcastr[e] (Tadcaster)
   Robert 39
Taliour, John, of Weighton 40
   see also Taylor
Tanfeld (Tanfield), Roger de 47
Tanfield, rector of
   see Norton, master William
Tawton
   William Carter of see Carter
Taylor, Taylour
   John 4
   John, of Tickhill 43,48
   see also Taliour
tenth of temporalities and spiritualities for the king's use 21
testaments
   see wills
Theobald, Br., O.Cist., monk at Scarborough 19
Terrington, rector of
   see Kyrketon, Thomas
Tesedale, Tesdale, Thesedale (Teesdale)
   Br. John de, monk of St Mary's, York 45
   Richard 33
   Richard [?the same] 43
   master Thomas 46
Thesedale
   see Tesedale
Thirletoft
   see Thryntoft
Thirnom, Robert, chaplain of St Mary's chantry, Goxhill 31
Thoresby, John, abp of York iii
Thornholm, John 7
Thornton Dale, rector of
   see Malton, Richard
Thornton in Craven
   rectors of see
      Popilton, Adam de
      Quik, Rowland
   rectory of 1,2

Thorp
   Br. Richard, canon of Malton 48
   William son of Roger de, of Burnsall 16
Thorpe by Bedale (?Thorpe Perrow) 18
Thryntoft, Thirletoft, Thryntoft (Thrintoft)
   Br. William, O.Carm., of Doncaster 43,44,49
Thwaythes, Thwates, del Thwayte
   Br. Richard, monk of Furness 43,44;
   monk of Calder 47
Thyrntoft
   see Thryntoft
Tickhill
   John Taylour of see Taylour
tithes, sale and farming of 16
Tolston, Richard 42
Tombarne, Juliana 13
Toppeclyff (Topcliffe)
   Br. Robert, monk of St Mary's, York 45
Torkesay (Torksey)
   Br. John, O.S.A. 46
Torksey, Lincs.
   priory of 42,46
Trotter, John 4
Tunstall, Br. William, monk of Fountains 45
Turnham Hall, pa. Hemingbrough 8
Twiford, prebend of, in St Paul's cathedral, London
   prebendaries of see
      Danby, master John
      Weston, master Thomas de
Twynan, Henry 38
Tymersholt (?for Tyversolt, i.e. Teversal), Robert de, vicar of Greasley 29
Ulverscroft, Leics.
   priory of 43,48
Umfray, Joan 28
Upholland, Lancs.
   priory of 42
Upton, Br. Roger de, vicar of Sheffield, prior of Worksop 37
vestments, benediction of ecclesiastical 3

vicar-general
   see Carleton, William [Norwich]
      Cawode, master William de
      [York]
   see also commissions
vicarages, admissions to 13,23,
   29,30,35,37
visitation of religious houses
   6,16
   injunctions 6
Wadmain, John 20
Wadworth
   vicarage of 13
   vicars of see
      Campsale, John de
      Maundeville, William
Wake, Br. Thomas, canon of
   Mattersey 45
Wakefeld (Wakefield), John 44
Waldby, Robert, abp of York
   passim
   missing register of iii-iv
   seal of, as abp of Dublin 1n,
     6n,8n
   seal of, as abp of York 15n
   vicar-general of see
      Cawode, master William de
Walden, pa. Barnoldswick 18
Walesby, Lincs.
   rectors of see
      Wayte, John
      Wilford, Thomas
Waleys, John 35
Walker, William 40,44,49
Wallingwells, Notts.
   prioress and convent of 10
Walton
   John Martill of see Martill
Walworth, master Thomas, canon
   of York 21
Wandesford, Wannesford (Wansford)
   Thomas 10
   Walter de 10
   William 8
Waplyngton (Waplington), Br.
   Thomas, O.Carth. of Hull 40,
   45
Ward, Br. Elias, O.F.M. 45
Wardall, Br. Robert de, canon of
   Malton 48
Warkesop (Worksop), Br. Richard
   de, subprior of Worksop 10
Warmsworth
   rector of see
      Kyndenesse, John
   rectory of 35

Warre, Warr
   master Thomas la,
   prebendary of Grindal
   [York], prebendary of
   Crophill and Oxton
   [Southwell] 23,24;
   prebendary of Lafford
   [Lincoln] 24n
Warter
   priory of 40,41,43,44,45,
   46,48,49
      canon of see
         Wartr[e], Br.
         William de
   see also Wartr[e]
Warton, John [de] 40,47
Wartr[e] (Warter)
   Br. Alan, O.Carm. 37,45,
   50
   Br. William de, canon of
   Warter 44
   see also Warter
Watton
   priory of 40,41,42,43,44,
   48,49
      canons of see
         Shalford, Br. John de
         Watton, Br. William
         de
   Br. William de, canon of
   Watton 42
   see also Whatton
Wayte, John, rector of
   Hickling, rector of
   Walesby 26
Weighton, (Market)
   Adam Patson of see Patson
   John Taliour of see
   Taliour
Welbeck, Notts.
   abbey of 40,44,49
      canons of see
         Billysthorp, Br.
         Simon
         Clyfton, Br. Benedict
         de
         Wortelay, Br. John de
Well, John at 4
Wellesede, Robert 4
Wellhaugh, Nbld.
   document dated at 15
Wells, Somerset
   cathedral church of
      vicarage in [?] 12 & n
      see also
         Axiholme, Peter

Wellys, Br. Robert, O.F.M. of
   Newcastle 42
   William 43
Welton
   see also Melton
Wencelawe (Wensley), John 42
Wenslay (Wensley), John, citizen
   of York 7
Westderby, Derby, Richard,
   archdeacon of Nottingham 25,
   27,28
Westminster
   abbey ii
   documents dated at 25,36
Weston, master Thomas de,
   prebendary of Twiford [London],
   prebendary of Darlington,
   prebendary of Crophill and
   Oxton [Southwell] 15,23,24;
   prebendary of Grindal [York] 24;
   archdeacon of Durham 24
Westwyk (Westwick), John de 48
Westyrdall (Westerdale)
   William de 43
Wetewang (Wetwang)
   Richard [de], rector of
   Dunnington 5,13
Wetherby, Br. John, monk of
   Whalley 40
Whallaye (Whalley), Br. William,
   monk of Whalley 40
Whalley, Lancs.
   abbot of 6
   monks of see
     Blakburn, Br. John
     Farmlaw, Br. Robert
     Keleby, Br. John
     Otryngton, Br. Robert
     Rysselay, Br. Thomas
     Skelton, Br. Gerard
     Wetherby, Br. John
     Whallaye, Br. William
Whatton, John, warden of St Mary's
   chantry, Sibthorpe, rector of
   Goxhill 14
   see also Watton
Whitby, abbot and convent of 23
   see also Whytby
Whitewell (Whitwell)
   John, provost of Kirkby
   Overblow 3
Whithorn, bishop of see
   Oswald, Br.
Whynfell (Whin Fell)
   John de 18
Whytby (Whitby)
   John [de] 41,45
Whyte, Thomas 46

Wilberfoss, priory of 41,43,
   45,46
Wilford, Wilforde, Wylford
   Thomas, rector of Walesby,
   rector of Hickling 26,27
wills 8,19,25,26,33,34
   probate of 8,16,17,19,22,
   23,25,26,29,30,33
Wode, Thomas 42
Wodhaw, John 39
Wodhorn (Woodhorn)
   Br. William, canon of
   Hexham 15
Wolton (Woolton), Thomas 27
Worcester, diocese of 24
Worcestr[e] (Worcester)
   Br. John, O.Carm. 39
   see also Wyrcetr[e]
Worksop, Notts.
   priory and convent of 37
   canon of see
     Brammelay, Br.Henry de
   prior of see
     Upton, Br. Roger de
   subprior of see
     Warkesop, Br.Richard de
Wortelay (Wortley)
   Br. John de, canon of
   Welbeck 41
Wresyll (Wressle)
   Henry, chaplain of the
   chantry at the altar of St
   John in the church of St
   Peter the Little, York 36
Wryde, John 41,46
Wryght
   John, of Nottingham 27
   Robert, of Fenton 41,46
   William, of Dunnington 47
Wygan (Wigan), Adam, rector of
   St Saviour, York 33
Wyghall (Wighill)
   Br. Thomas, O.Carm. 40
Wylson, Adam 4
Wymton [unidentified]
   John Clerk de see Clerk
Wyndell, Thomas, of Poppleton
   38,42
Wykeham, priory of 49
Wyrcetr[e] (Worcester)
   Br. John, canon of Malton 48
Wyverthorp (Weaverthorpe)
   Thomas 47
Yllyngworth
   see Illyngworth
York
   abbey of St Mary's 21

York
  abbey of St Mary's
    monks of see
      Tesdale, Br.John de
      Toppeclyff, Br.Robert
  archbishop of
    bailiff of 2
    palace of, at 12
    registers of iii-iv,9,
    10,12,22n,37
    steward of 2,5
    suffragans of see
      Oswald, Br., bp of
      Whithorn
      Richard, Br., episcopus
      Serviensis
    vicar-general of see
      Cawode, master William de
    see also under
      Arundel, Thomas
      Bowet, Henry
      Melton, William
      Neville, Alexander
      Scrope, Richard
      Thoresby, John
      Waldby, Robert
  archdeacon of
    official of 1,3,6,28,30,
    35,36,37
  archdeaconry of 2,3
    penitentiary in see
      Sparowe, Robert
  Austin friars of see
    Blake, Br. Robert
    Duffelde, Br. Robert
  Carmelite friars of see
    Boston, Br. William
    Byrden, Br. John
    Stepyng, Br. John
    Swyneshede, Br. Adam
  cathedral church of St Peter 21,
  41,42,43,44,45,47,49
    canons of see
      Feryby, master Nicholas de
      Walworth, master Thomas
    chapter of 2,13,20,24,25,28,
    chapter-house of 37
    dean of 20
    dean and chapter of 20
    parsons of see
      Darnyngton, John
      Sparowe, Robert
    prebend of see
      Grindal
    prebendaries of see
      Warre, master Thomas la
      Weston, master Thomas de

York
  cathedral church of St Peter (cont.)
    treasurer of see
      Newton, John de
    vicar choral of see
      Popilton, John de
    vicarage in 38,39
      see also
      Feriby, Robert
      Killom, Thomas
  chapel of St Mary and the
  Holy Angels 12,36
    prebendaries of see
      Neuton, William de
      Popilton, Thomas
  church of St Crux 46
    see also Tesdale,
    master Thomas
  church of St Michael le
  Belfrey 10
  church of St Peter the
  Little
    chantry at the altar of
    St John the Baptist
    in 36
      chaplains of see
        Pykton, John de
        Wresyll, Henry
    rector of see
      Assburn, Robert
  church of St Saviour
    rector of see
      Wygan, Adam
  citizens of see
    Manchestr[e], Thomas
    Wenslay, John
  city of 1,3
  Convocation of the province
  of 21,32
  diocese of 1,9,15,24,26,
  27,32,33,34,36
  documents dated at 7,8,
  9,10,11,12,13,14,16,17,
  18,19,21,22,31,32,33,34,
  35,36
  Dominican friars of see
    Chadburn, Br. John
    Godeworth, Br. Henry
    Hert, Br. Alan de
    Myrtford, Br. Thomas de
    Oliver, Br. Robert
    Raylay, Br. John
    Segesfeld, Br.Thomas de
  hospital of St Leonard 38,
  40,41,44,45,46,50
    conventual church of 9,
    39

York
    hospital of St Mary, Bootham   37,
    38,41,45,46,47,48
    hospital of St Thomas the Martyr
    outside Micklegate Bar   14
    priory of Clementhorpe   37,38,40,
    41,42,43,45,46,48,49
    priory of Holy Trinity, Micklegate
        conventual church of   37,38,43
    priory of St Andrew   40,41,45,46,49
    John Midelham of <u>see</u>
        Midelham
Yrchestr[e] (Irchester)
    Br. Thomas, O.S.A.   44
Ʒork, Thomas   46